The Rising of Bread for the World

An Outcry of Citizens Against Hunger

Arthur Simon

Paulist Press
New York/Mahwah, NJ

Cover design by Sharyn Banks
Book design by Lynn Else

Library of Congress Cataloging-in-Publication Data

Simon, Arthur R.
    The rising of Bread for the World : an outcry of citizens against hunger / Arthur Simon.
        p. cm.
    ISBN 978-0-8091-4600-0 (alk. paper)
    1. Bread for the World (Organization) 2. Hunger—Religious aspects—Christianity. 3. Food supply—Religious aspects—Christianity. 4. Church work with the poor. I. Title.
    BR115.H86S56 2009
    261.8´32606073—dc22

2008052711

Published by Paulist Press
997 Macarthur Boulevard
Mahwah, New Jersey, 07430

www.paulistpress.com

Printed and bound in the
United States of America

Table of Contents

Acknowledgments v

A Preliminary Word vii

  1. Growing Up in Oregon..1

  2. To the Midwest 14

  3. Theology and Politics...25

  4. Pastoral Formation 33

  5. New York's Lower East Side 43

  6. Poverty and Civil Rights 53

  7. Encountering Hunger...64

  8. Launching Bread for the World...74

  9. Watching It Rise 83

 10. The Right to Food 90

 11. The Fight for Food..101

 12. Hunger at Home...109

 13. Moving to Washington..115

 14. Setbacks and Successes 125

 15. Changing of the Guard...139

 16. Transforming the Politics of Hunger 148

 17. Retrospect and Prospect 161

Acknowledgments

I thank, first of all, those who helped me in the founding of Bread for the World, and everyone since then whose participation has made Bread for the World possible. I mention only a few in this book. A host of others have made exceptional contributions on our board or staff, as activists, donors, or members of Congress. I can't put into adequate words how grateful I am to them and for them. I am pained not to credit each by name.

Among those neglected, I think of staff members who helped build Bread and went on to make exceptional contributions elsewhere. To give you but a sampling: Steve Coats, my first administrative assistant, and later director of policy analysis, now with the U.S. Labor Education in the Americas Project; Kim Bobo, a young organizer, and then our director of organizing, who met and married Steve at Bread, and who is now the founding director of the National Interfaith Committee for Worker Justice; Christine Pohl of our Institute staff, now author and professor of Christian ethics at Asbury Theological Seminary; Kimble Forrester, organizer, now founding director of Alabama Arise!; Pat Nalls, on our support staff, who founded and directs the Women's Collective, an HIV-AIDS group; and John Prendergast, policy analyst, now with the International Crisis Group, frequently interviewed on network television about Darfur or other crises in the Horn of Africa. These give you only a hint of the talents offered to Bread by many others.

I also thank those who read all or parts of an early draft of this book and offered useful suggestions: Harold Remus (who has done this for all of my books), Bob and Marla Lichtsinn, Barbara Howell, Jennifer Coulter-Stapleton, David Beckmann, Steve Miller, Glenys Becker, Kitty Schaller, and Shirley Simon. In addition, Michelle

Learner and Sophie Milam tracked down statistics for me. I am grateful to them as well.

All royalties for the sale of this book are going to Bread for the World, a collective Christian voice urging our nation's decision makers to end hunger at home and abroad. For more information, contact:

Bread for the World
50 F Street NW Ste 500
Washington, DC 20001
Phone: 1-800-82-BREAD
www.bread.org

A Preliminary Word

A cartoon pictures a couple of cultured gentlemen at an upscale reception, each holding a drink as they converse. One of them says, "But enough about you. Let's talk about *me*."

As an autobiographical story, this book is by definition an exercise in "talking about me," and that puts me on dangerous turf. Jesus warned against those who do things in order to be seen by others. "They *have* their reward," Jesus observed. The effort amounts to nothing but puffery in God's eyes.

On the pages that follow, my aim is to tell how my story has a bearing on that of Bread for the World, the nation's foremost citizens' lobby on hunger. I place Bread's launching and development in the context of my own life and of the ways in which advantages and circumstances conspired to give me a special role in its birth and early development—always with unseen guidance and help from others much wiser than I. Although I meant my part in it to be an offering to God, clearly it was first and foremost God's gift to me.

I see the slices of my life as preparation for a larger work of God; for I believe Bread for the World to be a reflection, however small and dim, of the love and justice of the Kingdom, evidence that God can use the simplest and weakest of us to do heaven's work on earth.

Part of that work is to release others from the scourge of hunger. God has already enabled the world to achieve dramatic gains against hunger within my lifetime, and we are within striking distance of ending the rest of it. The pages that follow show how this might be done. They tell how ordinary people, by raising their collective voice to the nation's decision makers, are already engaged in making it happen.

1

Growing Up in Oregon

My birth in Eugene, Oregon, on July 28, 1930, defied the doctors. Soon afterward, my mother was found to have a tumor in her uterus and needed a hysterectomy. The surgeon told her that he did not understand how she had been able to give birth, but there I was, a six-pound child of a young Lutheran pastor and his wife. The only surprise to them at the time was my gender. My brother Paul had arrived twenty months earlier, and my parents were so confident God would balance the family with a girl that they had already chosen "Arlene" as a name. "Arthur" emerged in a rush to correct that mistake.

Unlikely as was my birth, it led to an even more unlikely life. Nothing in my imagination as a youth or a young adult came remotely close to anticipating the way in which my life unfolded. So the story I tell is that of an ordinary clay pot put to unexpected use.

Both of my parents grew up in German-speaking homes. My father, Martin, was born in 1903, ten months before the Wright brothers flew the first successful power-driven airplane. He was the second of nine children of Traugott and Eleanor (Elbert) Simon, a devout Lutheran couple who farmed eighty acres near Bonduel, Wisconsin, and who provided a home of extraordinary love. At age twelve, with sights already on the ministry, Dad entered a Lutheran prep school and junior college in Milwaukee and from there advanced to Concordia Seminary, St. Louis.

My mother, Ruth, had a less promising start. In 1907, abandoned as a newborn infant in Marshalltown, Iowa, she was taken to a Lutheran orphanage in Fort Dodge and after seven months transferred to a similar institution in St. Louis, where a middle-aged couple, Julius and Sophie Tolzmann, adopted her. When my mother was three-years old, Sophie died of meningitis. Two years later Julius

1

killed himself, apparently depressed over the loss of his wife and the fact that his work as a bookkeeper denied him the ability to provide a home for little Ruth. She had already been taken in by Sophie's older sister, Emilie Troemel, fifty-two, and her husband Gustav, sixty-two, who owned a bakery in St. Louis. They had an unhappy marriage, their children were already grown, and an emotionally troubled Emilie frequently reminded my mother that her presence was an intrusion.

During my father's last year in St. Louis, he and my mother met at a seminary basketball game. They were married in September 1926, he at age twenty-three, she nineteen. Two weeks after the wedding they boarded a ship for China, where my father had been "called," as he desired, to be a missionary. My mother was eager to get away from home, and China seemed about the right distance.

They studied language for some months in Shanghai and Wuhan (Hankow), but settled in Wanxian, about 1,200 miles up the Yangtze River, where my father began to preach in the Mandarin language. However, the Communist uprising prompted the mission board of the Missouri Synod (a conservative national Lutheran body) to order the temporary return of missionaries with young children or pregnant wives. My mother was carrying Paul, so they came back to the States, expecting to be reassigned to China. Missionary colleagues asked my father to represent them regarding a disagreement they had with the St. Louis–based mission board over which Chinese word to use for "God." He did so, but as a consequence the board refused to return him to China.

My father then accepted an invitation to serve Grace Lutheran Church in Eugene, Oregon, where Paul and I were born. Eugene had a population of 19,000 at the time, compared to more than 150,000 now. But nearly eighty years prior to my birth, Eugene was a wilderness with a population near zero, not counting the Kalapuya Indians who hunted elk there: so rapidly did change occur in the span of two lifetimes.

The parsonage in which we lived had been a small farmhouse, now nestled just five blocks from the heart of Eugene's main street in one direction and the same distance in the opposite direction from the University of Oregon. Our backyard had a plum and prune tree, a gooseberry bush, lilac bushes, walnuts from a neighbor's tree, and

Dad's vegetable garden. We lived behind a stately white wooden church with an immense steeple that creaked when the wind blew. In this church my father preached. The people I got to know and love most gathered on Sundays and sometimes between. The parsonage frequently welcomed visitors, some of them parishioners who brought food, and others unemployed transients who sought food.

The house and the church were the center of our family life, both of them places of prayer. Family devotions followed every supper. We memorized lengthy sections from the Bible, such as entire psalms or the Beatitudes, by the simple method of saying a verse in unison and adding a line each evening. Then Dad would read or tell a Bible story and ask questions that helped us connect the stories to daily life. He had a great gift for this. Before bedtime we sat on his lap and he would tell stories from the Bible or, just as often, make up kids' adventures that required some kind of divine intervention. Dad's stories fascinated and shaped us. He always made sure to include God's love and forgiveness in Christ, and our obligation to love others. He maintained that a child in a Christian home should grow up from infancy with trust in Jesus as the Savior, and that trust became the foundation of our lives.

Dad's own life reinforced this. Someone said, "He is as nice to his kids as he is to guests," and that was true. He once told us, "Even the cows should know you are a Christian by the way you treat them."

During his first two years in Eugene, Dad had no car, so he visited members and prospective members by walking, taking a city bus, or being picked up and driven to homes. About the time of my birth in 1930, he bought a Model A Ford, which served us beyond my sixteenth birthday. The congregation grew, and when I was about six years old, Dad told us that the members had voted to increase his salary to $84 a month. I was astonished. It seemed to me as though we had struck it rich—and we had, but not in the way I understood.

Christmas was the highlight of the church year for me in those days. During Advent the Sunday school practiced for the children's Christmas service. On Christmas Eve, with a towering tree brightly sparkling and the church packed, we sang songs for the congregation, and each child had a verse to recite alone—scary but exciting. One song began, "As each happy Christmas dawns on earth again." I was four or five years old and wondered what an "azzie chappy" Christmas was, but never asked. I accepted it as one of the mysteries of God. Another mystery for me: How did God get all the money that we collected for him on Sundays? As you can see, I had no special aptitude for theology. But I did enjoy Christmas, and though our presents were few, my delight was great.

I am surprised now at the freedom that our parents allowed us at an early age, perhaps because life was, in many respects, simpler and safer then. When I was five-years old I saw my first movie, and Paul and I were allowed to walk unaccompanied to the Mayflower Theater several blocks down the street. That movie starred Shirley Temple, and my little heart was totally smitten. When the movie was over, Paul said, "Let's go home." I refused. He left and I stayed to see it again. I had to walk home in the dark by myself, where a spanking awaited me—but Shirley Temple was worth it.

By the time I was seven and Paul nine, our parents would on rare occasions go out for the evening and trust us to behave ourselves without a baby sitter. One evening, with strict instructions to be in bed by eight thirty, we turned our house into a basketball court with the help of a tennis ball and a couple of waste baskets. Eight thirty came too soon, so we set the clock back an hour. It was not a perfect crime, however, because we forgot to set the clock forward again. We seldom got spanked, but that time the punishment fit the crime.

Expanding the Ministry

Not long after arriving in Eugene, Dad began taking graduate courses and eventually earned a doctorate in education at the university. He focused on child rearing and family life. Sensing a need in our Sunday school, he urged Concordia Publishing House in St. Louis to create a four-page weekly handout for Sunday school kids, but CPH declined. So with the help of a local printer, Dad started *The Children's Hour*. It had purpose-driven stories, jokes, advice, and dot-to-dot drawings. He got orders from other congregations and before long began sending out thousands of copies each week. He divided our garage in half, poured a cement floor on one side to hold equipment, and soon did his own printing. His next initiative was a monthly magazine, *The Christian Parent*, that featured family devotions and articles on child rearing.

These initiatives flourished with the encouragement of the congregation, but Dad's editing and publishing began to overtake his efforts to nourish a growing church. He decided to resign as pastor in order to devote his full time to his family-life ministry, so in the summer of 1938 we moved into a house on a sparsely settled hillside a few blocks west of town. The house had been owned by the Rose Bud Bakery, and its bakery stood behind the house. The bakery became our print shop with extensions added as subscriptions grew.

All of this meant big changes for us. For one thing Dad's work was a do-or-die family enterprise and we all had to pitch in. Mom typed rapidly and knew how to handle office details. Paul and I were required to put in one hour a day on school days and three hours on Saturdays as our contribution to the family. Beyond that we earned fifteen cents an hour. We learned how to fold papers fast; how to assemble, staple, and cut magazines; and eventually how to set type and run presses. We enjoyed doing these things most of the time. We saw Dad manage a growing business, watched him pound away at his typewriter, and heard him lecture. I now realize how influential Dad's initiatives and Mom's dogged support were in shaping our careers, leading Paul to the U.S. Senate and me to the launching of Bread for the World.

That summer I started wearing glasses. The first eight years of my life I had terrible vision and didn't realize it until Paul complained of headaches and Mom decided to have our eyes tested. It turned out that my vision was much worse than Paul's. When my glasses came and I put them on, I was amazed to discover how different the world looked. People were no longer fuzzy. I could see individual leaves on trees and blades of grass. The world hadn't changed, of course, but my ability to see the world had. Decades later it dawned on me that this is a picture of our life in Christ. Entering that new reality does not change the world, but it changes the way we see the world. We begin to view ourselves, others, and all creation as we truly are: through the eyes of God. Imperfectly, of course. Ours is a lifelong journey of learning to see through the heart and mind of Christ—a far bigger change than getting a new pair of glasses.

Other changes included making new friends, among them the Norman Pohll family, our neighbors with whom we established life-long ties. They had been members of our church, and had a large grocery store nearby. Young Norm and I played together a lot, roaming the countryside, and enjoying friendly fights with an endless supply of fir cones that lay in wooded areas. The move also put us in a three-room school with eight grades, a thought that alarmed Paul and me because we had been told that country schools weren't as good as city schools. But Dunn School turned out to be better, at least for us. It required a walk of more than a mile each way, and in western Oregon that often meant walking in the rain. The school had a nice community feel to it and devoted teachers, so we were blessed.

During the 1938–39 school year, when I was in the third grade, the University of Oregon won the nation's first NCAA basketball championship. The previous year Oregon had an outstanding team, and for twenty-five cents a ticket Paul and I attended many of the home games. We were hooked. The next year almost all the same players returned, and Oregon methodically took the conference title; beat California, Texas, and Oklahoma for the coast and regional titles; and finally beat Ohio State for the national championship. We were ecstatic, glued to the radio for each game. We cheered them in the victory parade. One Saturday, Paul and I biked to the campus, tracked down all ten players, and got their autographs. By then the only imaginable goal in life for this short and skinny little kid was to play basketball for Oregon.

Years later, while visiting Oregon around the time of my sixty-fifth birthday, I arranged to see each of the four players from that team who were still alive: All-Americans Laddie Gale and John Dick, as well as Bob Hardy and Ford Mullen. All four were gracious hosts and I had a great time listening to them talk about the team and their memories of that year. Getting to spend a couple of hours with each allowed me to recapture a boyhood dream. But that wasn't all. The day I turned sixty-five I visited MacArthur Court, the basketball arena where I had seen all those games. The doors were locked, but along came a delivery man who allowed me to slip inside, where I found a student playing ball. I took off my shoes and for the first time stood on the court and shot baskets where my heroes had once played. I made a few, missed quite a few, and then finally swished a three-pointer. I hope you will understand that despite the empty bleachers, I heard the crowd roar as I walked off that court.

Dunn School's main competitive sport was softball, and I owe my part in it to the thoughtfulness of Johnny Dunn, a local semipro baseball star. When I was in the sixth grade, Dunn became the school's principal and its teacher of grades seven and eight. He announced tryouts, but I started down the road for home. Mr. Dunn asked me why I wasn't trying out, and I told him I wasn't good enough. He said, "Come on anyway and we'll see." He showed some of us how to catch fly balls. I developed a knack for turning my back to the ball and running to the end of its trajectory for the catch. To my surprise Mr. Dunn placed me in right field (where the fewest balls land), and the following year in center field. Then he taught me how to pitch windmill style, so during the summer before eighth grade, I spent an hour each day working on speed and accuracy. We had some fine athletes on the team, including a friend I still keep in touch with, Ed Ziniker, a talented catcher. That year we beat every team we played.

Sport was a passion for me in grade school, but other influences—family, church, friends, and relatives—were deeper and more enduring. My parents rank first, of course, with Paul next. He was the leader, the "grade skipper," the "people person." His interest in things stimulated mine. At the age of twelve he spoke of editing a weekly newspaper and going into politics. He had read the autobiography of William Allen White, editor of *The Emporia Gazette* in Kansas, who used his newspaper to comment on national issues, and I'm sure that influenced Paul.

"But what will you do when you run for sheriff and lose?" Dad asked him.

"I won't lose," Paul replied.

My father sighed.

Paul and I quarreled about things like who was stacking more than his share of the firewood along the side of the garage or who was hogging the larger half of our bed. But most of the time we enjoyed doing things together. When Paul entered a local contest to see who could collect and donate the most pairs of usable old shoes (a Depression-era need), it became a family project, and Paul won the coveted prize: a Silver King bicycle.

I'm sorry that as a child I didn't get to know far-away relatives better. We did see some of them occasionally, but only later in life did I discover how interesting most of them are. My cousins and their children have had a wide range of careers, but excel most of all in being enjoyable company. Dad's young cousin Lynn Simon had a farm near Salem and was later said to be the largest bell-pepper grower on the West Coast. When he died, the family had his casket covered with green onions, bell peppers, and roses.

One absent relative became a vivid presence in our lives. Aunt Gertrude, Dad's older sister and a deaconess-nurse, had followed him to China, where she spent the rest of her life. A charismatic personality, Aunt Gertrude was first and foremost an evangelist, who introduced many to Christ. "When you marry, be sure to marry a Galatians 2:20* Christian," she advised me. She embodied the advice except that she never married; however, she informally adopted more than a dozen discarded children. She was also among the last Americans to flee to Hong Kong when the Communists came to power. There, instead of returning home as instructed, she started a Bible school in Rennie's Mill Camp, a hillside that was covered with shacks cobbled together by a vast population of destitute refugees. The Bible school eventually merged with a seminary, and today a large, thriving prep school, grades seven through thirteen, is named after her.

When Aunt Gertrude visited us on furlough, she would mesmerize me and the Sunday school with her stories and zeal for Jesus. Because the Missouri Synod would not permit women to preach, Dad would have her address the congregation without using the pulpit—a fig leaf to circumvent policy. Aunt Gertrude's impulsiveness gave the mission board fits. With no patience for bureaucratic procedure, she would see an opportunity, take action, and then insist that the board catch up. She finally severed ties with the board in order to foster indigenous leaders faster than the board would allow, and she soldiered on until cancer took her.

---

* I have been crucified with Christ, and it is no longer I who live, but it is Christ who lives in me. And the life I now live in the flesh I live by faith in the Son of God, who loved me and gave himself for me (Gal 2:19–20).

War Years

Upon arriving home from church one Sunday in 1941, we heard on the radio the stunning announcement that the Japanese had attacked Pearl Harbor. We were at war. I was old enough at eleven to sense that momentous changes lay ahead. I felt mainly excitement— a reaction that suggests why war so often seems adventurous to those far removed from its horror. I soon got a wake-up call when we heard that Wilma, one of Dad's young employees, had lost her fiancé at Pearl Harbor when the USS *Arizona* sank. I didn't know what to say to her, so I said nothing, but wondered at her grief. One by one the young men in our congregation, some just out of high school, were called to serve in the armed forces. We got only snippets of information about them, though occasionally one would show up in uniform. I had only the vaguest idea of what they were going through.

Our congregation was grateful not to have lost a man, but I am surprised at how little we tapped their experiences for our own instruction when they returned home. Did they feel ignored, or were they pleased not to have us poke deep wounds? I think their stories would have given us an invaluable dose of reality. Years later, Ed Sullivan—not the TV star, but one of the fellows I admired most, wrote *Memoirs of a World War II Medic*,* a warmly human but sobering snapshot of war. I got another sobering snapshot on the fiftieth anniversary of D-day when I invited a friend, Andy Coverston, for dinner to hear his account of the initial landing. He spoke of wading toward shore, bullets and shrapnel flying everywhere, when the fellow next to him got hit and slipped into the water. Andy pulled him up, but the soldier told him to let go and keep moving, as they had been ordered to do. So Andy let him slump back into the ocean and continued ashore. "Did I do the right thing?" he asked. For fifty years the question had haunted him.

World War II gave me my main lessons in geography. I followed developments in Europe as the German army marched into one country after another. My prayers that Norway would defeat the Nazis were not answered, certainly not in the way I intended, and

---

* Ed Sullivan, *Memoirs of a World War II Medic* (Springfield, OR), 2002.

this put me in a quandary about the nature of prayer. With war suddenly expanding in the Pacific region and our own country fully engaged, I followed daily reports and maps in *The Eugene Register-Guard* as avidly as I read the sports page and the comics.

Dad set an example for us during the war. Anti-Japanese sentiment in the United States was rife, and nowhere more intense than on the West Coast. We had blackout drills in Eugene to prepare ourselves for the possibility of Japanese bombers. The lyrics of some popular songs showed deep contempt for the Japanese. Many of us feared that West Coast facilities might be targets of subversive acts by Japanese American citizens. So about ten weeks after Pearl Harbor, on February 19, 1942, President Roosevelt signed an executive order to imprison all people of Japanese descent on the West Coast in detention camps. It was a popular but shameful decision. In a sermon broadcast on KORE, the local radio station, my father spoke against it. He also wrote a letter of protest to the *Register-Guard*. These actions attracted vocal critics, including a few from our church, but Dad stood his ground. My friends were oblivious to this, but some of Paul's demanded an explanation.

Exactly sixty-five years after Roosevelt's order, a memorial to Oregon's contingent of those 120,000 honorable citizens was dedicated at the civic center in Eugene, on the spot where many of them had been rounded up. It includes a stone with this inscription:

IN TRIBUTE TO
Rev. Martin P. Simon
He spoke in protest.
His courage inspired others.

High School

After my confirmation and eighth-grade graduation, Dad wanted me to attend Concordia prep school in Portland, hoping I would prepare for the pastoral ministry. I didn't want to go because I had no intention of becoming a pastor. We finally compromised with the agreement that I would attend one year, and then if I wished, I could transfer to Eugene High. Concordia—now a university—was a high school with forty students. Except for a small gymnasium, everything was located in an old, wooden, three-story building. The top floor was a single room with beds from one end to the other. The first two floors housed everything else. My classes included German and Latin, plus the usual ninth-grade courses. Our four professors were highly competent, three of them old and strict. Most of the students expected to become pastors or teachers in the Lutheran Church, but some came because they had gotten in trouble at home. It was not always easy to tell the difference between the two. Concordia's tradition included hazing, which was not much fun for a freshman, but not too bad if you pretended to think well of it.

I transferred to Eugene High School as a sophomore. It seemed huge, almost a thousand students. Two memories stand out: The first was getting permission to take Julia Gibson's creative writing class, which was normally reserved for juniors and seniors. I wanted to be a writer. In eighth grade I had started writing a Tom Sawyer–inspired novel and got part way before laying it aside. I still have it: twenty-seven pages written with pencil in small letters on narrow-lined paper. If I had finished it and gotten help from an editor, it might have worked. At any rate, Miss Gibson's class challenged me and furthered my interest in writing.

The second memory has to do with the Hi-Y Club, a Christian club, or perhaps a social club with a Christian intention. I wanted to join as a way of getting better acquainted. Dad did not want me to join because, as it still does, the Missouri Synod stood firmly against prayer-fellowship with Christians who belong to church bodies that differ with it on doctrine (which means just about everyone else). That isn't a humble position, but Dad thought it ought to be observed. He finally gave in when I argued that Fred Dodge, who belonged to our church, was student chaplain of the Hi-Y that year, so I really would be praying with one of our own. That gave him another fig leaf and gave me membership in the Hi-Y.

You might assume from what I have written so far that I was an extrovert. That was true at home and with a handful of people I knew well. With them I was a noisy kid. But with strangers and groups, I was painfully shy. To stand in front of the class and recite anything scared me. When I became pitcher of our softball team, one of the teachers told my father, "Maybe it will help him overcome his inferiority complex." One of my worst moments came in the third grade: I had skipped singing with my class for a PTA performance, because the Oregon basketball team was playing away from home and I wanted to hear the broadcast. Defying the separation of church and state, Mrs. Taylor assigned penance by making me memorize a four-verse poem, "Jeremy Mouse." That part was okay, but I then had to knock on the door of the seventh- and eighth-graders room and tell Mrs. Rogers, the principal, I was there to recite a poem to her class. Of course, the seventh- and eighth-graders grinned from ear to ear while watching me twist in the wind.

Why was I so shy? Unlike Paul, who inherited and copied Dad's supreme confidence, I think I absorbed some of the insecurity Mom felt from her childhood. I say this not in blame, because she did a heroic job of rising above the emotional scars she carried. While Paul was all Dad, there was both a streak of Dad and a streak of Mom in me, and with crowds and strangers the latter prevailed. Being shy is not sinful, but it's not fun either.

In my longing not to be shy, I had the advantage of Dad and Paul as models, and much practice not being shy with friends, perhaps to their regret. I began paying more attention to my appearance. This included commendable things like combing my hair and shining my shoes, but less-commendable ones like metal wedges in heels so you could click them and be noticed when you walked. (I click, therefore I am.) Shedding shyness is like shedding weight, not meant to be done overnight.

Two developments gave my wobbly ego a boost. The first was an invitation to be the emcee at a banquet welcoming the new confirmation class into our church's high-school youth group, the Walther League. I was flabbergasted. Had they no idea how scared I was in front of groups? They apparently mistook private noise for public confidence. Dad always wove jokes and humorous stories into his lectures, so I tapped his file for some of those and thought of a few others I could use against people who had to be introduced. I arrived at the banquet a trembling puppy. I told the first story. The crowd laughed—hard. A sense of elation swept over me. I felt completely at ease, a feeling I had never before experienced in front of a group. The rest of the evening was pure fun. Of course, that event didn't end my jitters, but it did tell me that public speaking was something I could learn to do and enjoy.

The second confidence builder was Camp Colton, a summer camp for the postconfirmation youth of our Lutheran churches in Oregon. I was almost fourteen and recently confirmed, and I didn't want to go to camp, but Paul insisted. The first night there I felt miserable, surrounded by chattering strangers in a crowded barracks. But the next day I met Kenny Trinklein who was also planning to start at Concordia prep in the fall, and we became good friends. Paul was well known at camp, so many campers went out of their way to be friendly to me. The following summer was even better. Kenny wasn't there, but I hit it off well with Dave Becker, son of the camp dean. Dave had one of the friendliest personalities I've ever known, and we got acquainted with everyone. For the first time in my life I felt popular. Three years of camp, plus occasional Lutheran youth events where Dave and I would get together, lifted my confidence in a way that was similar to the lift I got at the confirmation banquet.

Popularity is fleeting and never safe. It meant more to me than it should have. But for this shy fellow, it was welcome assurance that life was bigger than I had imagined, and it helped me look forward. It also gave me the courage to invite Ruthie Maier, the pastor's daughter, to a youth banquet one September evening before our family said good-bye to Eugene and rolled out of town in our new 1946 Plymouth toward Southern Illinois.

2

To the Midwest

The new Plymouth, which sped at 50 miles an hour when traffic on two-lane highways permitted, came to us by the kindness of our neighbors Norman and Beryl Pohll, who gave us their place near the front of a long line of people waiting for new cars after World War II. I left Eugene with mixed emotions, sad about leaving the people and places I loved, but excited about the adventure of a new life in far-away Illinois. Dad told us that the growth of his ministry required a location closer to the population center of his magazine subscribers, who were primarily Missouri Synod Lutherans. That put God firmly on the side of moving, so protesting never occurred to me. Paul came along as well. Still seventeen, he had finished his first year at the University of Oregon and planned to transfer to the University of Illinois. But Illinois had a waiting list of former GIs, so Paul decided to attend Dana for a year, a Danish Lutheran college near Omaha, and then transfer. After dropping him off, we drove on to Illinois.

With a population of 4,000, Highland, Illinois, was located thirty-five miles east of St. Louis, just off Highway 40. Many of its residents were descendents of early Swiss settlers. A well-kept town, it had attracted my parents' interest, so they arranged to build our new office and printing plant there. We rented a small five-room flat on the second floor of an old two-story house a few blocks away.

We arrived in September after school had already started, so I entered the eleventh grade at Highland High as a conspicuous outsider—the most difficult part of the move for me. A week or so after we arrived, Ed Hilbert, the basketball coach and history teacher, raised the question of whether or not the school was friendly. He caught me off guard by saying, "You're new here, Art. What do you think? Do you like it here?" For a moment I froze. I wanted to say,

"No, I'm miserable and miss Eugene." That would have marked me as an outcast, so I quickly mustered the cowardice to lie with a bit of enthusiasm. "Yes," I said, "I like it here. People are very friendly." In fact, they *were* friendly, but a strange thing happened. Affirmation of their friendliness made it easier for me to approach them. Before long I was having a good time getting acquainted.

Highland High School had only two hundred students, and our class sixty. The size suited me well for easing into activities. Cheerleaders were desperate for another male—any male, no tryouts necessary they told me—and since I was desperate for social life, I accepted. Those were the days when the spectators yelled the cheers, and cheerleaders merely coaxed them with a few synchronized motions. The school also needed someone to edit the newspaper my senior year, which gave me an opportunity I probably would not have had in Eugene.

Two books during those high-school years, both gifts from Dad, made a huge impression on me. One was a copy of the Revised Standard Version of the New Testament, published in 1946. For the first time the four Gospels and the collection of letters came alive to me, and I read them from beginning to end. Even the format, in book style, gave the New Testament a contemporary feel.

The second book was *My Neighbor of Another Color*,* by Andrew Schulze. It was a shocking description of racism within the church—our *own* church body—with graphic examples of prejudice and discrimination that violated the Gospel. Schulze was a frail, gentle man with the mind of Christ, which gave him the courage of a saint. He served as pastor of St. Phillip's Lutheran Church, a black congregation in St. Louis, where in 1943 he founded the first Lutheran race-relations organization (and later the Lutheran Human Relations Association of America), which stirred awareness and fostered changes within the Missouri Synod. Dad and Mom were among the early members and I went with them to its annual conferences.

I soon found an opportunity to "do something" through our Lutheran youth organization in southern Illinois, where the crowning pleasure for me each year was a couple of weeks of summer camp in Pere Marquette State Park, overlooking the Illinois River. No

---

* Andrew Schulze, *My Neighbor of Another Color* (Minneapolis: Augsburg, 1944).

African Americans (or Negroes, as we said then) had ever attended camp, even though there was a black Lutheran congregation in nearby Alton, where Elijah Lovejoy, a Presbyterian minister and the nation's first journalist-martyr, had been murdered by a mob for his abolitionist views. So I arranged scholarships for two black teenagers from the Alton church. It was an easy, simple thing to do and, although I heard a bit of grumbling around the edges, Porter and Nikki were warmly accepted in what was probably their first experience of being popular among whites—a rare occurrence in the late 1940s, prior to the flowering of the civil rights movement. I wonder if they knew what they contributed to the rest of us.

After high-school graduation in 1948, I packed my suitcase and hitchhiked two thousand miles back to Oregon to visit friends in Eugene. Upon my return I spent the rest of the summer with Paul in Troy, a small town between Highland and St. Louis. During his third year of college, Paul had learned of an opportunity to buy a defunct weekly newspaper in Troy from a publisher dying of cancer, whose print shop stood there gathering dust. The Lions Club, which acted as a chamber of commerce, sought a buyer and heard of Paul's interest through my father. With an unsecured loan from the local bank, Paul bought the paper for $3,600, and at the age of nineteen became the youngest newspaper publisher in the nation.

Paul had worked two years part-time in the sports department of *The Eugene Register-Guard*, and both of us had grown up in Dad's print shop. But the equipment in the Troy print shop was primitive. When it ran, the 1879 Cranston press shook the old wooden building. Headlines had to be set by hand, one letter at a time. That printing process was technologically closer to Gutenberg's fifteenth-century invention than to modern offset printing. The linotype was old. A layer of thick dust covered everything, and giant roaches scampered for cover whenever we entered the front door after dark.

Our inexperience soon became evident. We managed, by working through the night, to get the first issue of *The Troy Tribune* ready for the press. The local high-school band was set to play across the street to celebrate delivery of the first copies. We poured ink in the press font, got ready to hand-feed huge sheets of paper, and turned on the power. The press made an awful, clankety racket but, to our delight, began to perform. (Nothing is sweeter than being on the verge of triumph.)

Suddenly, to our dismay, the old gelatin rollers that distribute the ink over the type crumbled. The inaugural issue had to wait a week so we could get the rollers refitted with new gelatin.

A humbling start it was, but perseverance paid off. Working all night before publication became routine. Roy Green, a friend of ours who worked for Paul that summer, quipped, "I knew I had to work forty hours a week, but I didn't know it was forty hours straight." Paul began to build a growing list of subscribers, secured advertisers, printed local personal news (which is the lifeblood of such papers), attended public meetings, and reported the needs, neglect, and progress on matters in Troy and throughout the county. Paul was getting an education, the paper was getting a good start, and I was getting ready for college.

Dana College

Paul spoke so highly of Dana College that I decided to go there too in the fall of 1948. I was not disappointed. What Dana lacked in academic credentials, it more than made up in small classes and dedicated faculty members. Above all, it provided a family atmosphere. With fewer than three hundred students, people got to know one another well. We had our meals in the dining hall of the women's dormitory. At the beginning of each week, we would draw numbers that assigned us to tables of six, a method that fostered the expansion of friendships. In the early evenings after dinner, students would hang out in the center of campus to visit and sing—popular songs, camp songs, and songs of faith. That probably sounds hopelessly old-fashioned to most readers, but I can tell you it was pure fun. It helped bring people together and build a feeling of solidarity.

Most students participated in campuswide social events, including football and basketball games. There were ample opportunities for specialized activities as well. For me, that included the men's glee club, and eventually the touring choir under the direction of Paul Neve, a genius at getting fine music out of mostly ordinary voices. Opportunities abounded, so I also took part in a couple of comedies and was active in the Lutheran Students Association. I probably did better socially than academically, which does me no particular credit. Almost upon arrival, I was asked (because of my brother's reputation) to lead a small group of Young Republicans. We did nothing but talk and wait for the inevitable election of Governor Thomas E. Dewey to the presidency in 1948. At breakfast the morning after Truman's victory in a historic upset, student Paul Johnsen banged on a metal pitcher to get attention and announced that I was convening a meeting of the Young Republicans in the nearest phone booth. Of course, the place cracked up. A couple of years later I wrote a column for the student newspaper defending Truman's firing of General MacArthur for insubordination, so my political leanings were evidently in flux.

During my second year at Dana, I served on the student council and was elected student-body president for the following year. When Paul and I were kids, my father used to tell us—sometimes in praise of someone and occasionally bemoaning inaction—that getting elected is not an honor but an opportunity. I thought I spotted an opportunity. Paul had served as student-body president at Dana three years earlier and gotten the college to adopt a stated policy of racial nondiscrimination, but there was resistance to implementation of that policy—not unusual in 1951. I learned that the Omaha Urban League had an outstanding young black leader, who was brilliant and an eloquent speaker, so I invited him to address the student body. Whitney Young—later executive director of the National Urban League and a major civil rights figure—spoke candidly but winsomely about racial discrimination in the nation and in the church. My sense was that students were deeply moved. I know I was.

Whitney Young's speech gave us an opening. The student council voted to propose to the student body that we gather funds toward the enrollment of a black student at Dana. The idea of getting student-body support for this was not entirely new, because for several years the student body had underwritten the support of a displaced person from Europe. Our scholar that year was Juri Taht, an Estonian who, after his father was killed by the Soviets, narrowly escaped to the West during the final stages of World War II. But would Dana's cautious president, R. E. Morton, agree to waive tuition for a black student, as the college had for the displaced persons, if the students raised money for living expenses?

I told President Morton that the student council had voted to sponsor another student and gather funds for that purpose and asked if the college would be willing to waive tuition once again. He assured me that it would. I did not specify that we intended to secure a black student this time. My lack of candor was not exactly honorable, though I did not lie. Next I called a meeting of the student body, which approved the council's proposal with no audible dissent. However, after learning the full intent of the student body, President Morton called me to his office and said I would have to get approval from the board of trustees. I wrote the trustees a full-page letter reporting that we had already collected enough money to provide for two black students if the trustees would allow free tuition. I urged them

> to make it clear once and for all where Dana stands on the race question. I have heard numerous reports—and I shall believe them to be false until I have evidence for assuming otherwise—that while the board has gone on record as opening the door to all races, in practice this is not encouraged. At our student body meeting several members reaffirmed this feeling....If you decide against this now, that point will be in doubt; if for it, your policy will be undebatably clear.*

I subsequently received a letter from President Morton informing me that the trustees had denied the student body's request on the grounds that forty tuition scholarships were already available to members of any race.

> The negro is an American citizen and has, in our part of the country, every right and opportunity that is available to whites. It is further the board's contention that just as the negro is entitled to and should have equality with the white race, so it is equally inconsistent to grant him opportunities and advantages which would make him a favored individual.†

---

* From an undated letter by the author to the Dana board of trustees prior to its meeting on April 4–5, 1951.
† From a letter, dated April 7, 1951, from R. E. Morton to the author.

Favored individual? The reply swept aside centuries of slavery, discrimination, and poverty, but students were determined, and they succeeded in bringing a black student to campus (the first of many) a year later, in the fall of 1952. Marion Hudson became a proud alumnus of Dana. He was a campus leader and a phenomenal athlete who earned 12 letters, scored 157 football points, and ran an average of 7.78 yards per carry during his four years at Dana. He won the broad jump and the javelin toss in the Drake relays and as a freshman scored more individual points at Drake than all of the Big Seven Conference teams combined. In 2003 he was celebrated at Dana with the creation of the Marion Hudson Scholarship, which is awarded each year in his honor.

Concordia Seminary

The summer after my first year at Dana became a turning point for me. I spent the first week or so hitchhiking to the East Coast with Ray Johnsen, a friend from Dana. Neither of us had previously seen New York or Washington. The trip was a memorable one and included our being escorted out of the Waldorf-Astoria Hotel, where we had dropped in as somewhat weather-beaten travelers to get a look. Ray spent the rest of the summer with Paul and me working on the newspaper. He found his future wife Nancy in Troy that summer, and their fifty-six years together have been one of the finest marriages I know.

The turning point for me occurred because, for the first time in my life, I wasn't sure what I wanted to do. I had thought seriously enough about journalism to check out a couple of weekly newspapers that were for sale in Missouri, and visited one of them. But the more I thought about it, the more I wondered if I was trying to replicate Paul's career. If so, would I not in all probability turn out to be a pale imitation? That left me wondering. I had changed my mind a few times in the past, but always because something came up that seemed better—like making your way across a stream by stepping from one stone to another, moving forward as the next stone came in sight. But now I felt as though I was stepping off a stone without having spotted another one to land on. I faced the age-old question, "How do you know God's will?" I didn't know, and it was not a good feeling.

I spent half the summer stewing about this, but also praying and talking to Paul. Gradually it seemed to me that while Paul felt called to serve God in public affairs as a layman, perhaps God was calling me to serve in the pastoral ministry. Dad used to tell us that whatever we decided to do in life was up to us, but the main thing was to do it for God. I had thought that not very helpful advice as a boy, but over the years it began to make more sense. So it happened that I decided to go to seminary and test out my desire to become a pastor. I told my father and he was pleased.

That decision meant taking courses in Greek, Latin, and German at Dana for a couple of years. I didn't know if Concordia Seminary in St. Louis would accept me, because it was still tied to an old German system of pre-seminary prep school with two years of college, then five years of seminary that included a year as an intern (or "vicar"). My credentials were thin, but Concordia had begun to be a little flexible. Several of us who entered seminary in the fall of 1951 had bypassed the prep schools and needed to do some language work on the side.

Concordia in St. Louis was the more open of the Missouri Synod's two seminaries, but was still conservative, which suited me fine. I arrived at a time when there were theological giants on the faculty. They included Jaroslav Pelikan, a twenty-seven-year-old prodigy who became arguably the world's foremost authority on the history of Christian thought. At the age of twenty-three, he had received his PhD from the University of Chicago and his divinity degree from Concordia Seminary on back-to-back weekends. His colleague Arthur Carl Piepkorn taught confessional and comparative theology. Both Pelikan and Piepkorn gave us an appreciation of Eastern and Roman Catholic traditions a decade before the Vatican II Council. Richard Caemmerer taught preaching with an unusually good understanding of the church in the world. The lectures of Martin Franzmann, a New Testament professor, made me imagine him as a famous German theologian. We also had run-of-the-mill professors, but the men named, as well as others, made us grateful. The student body had its own promising talent that included Martin

Marty, later the prolific church historian. He edited *The Seminarian*, our theological students' journal. These names only scratch the surface. It was a place to cherish, one that challenged us to believe and to think—with a Lutheran focus on justification by grace, through faith, of course.

Paul Jersild, who had been my roommate at Dana, and I decided to hitchhike around Europe the summer following my first year at the seminary. One attraction was the Lutheran World Federation assembly in Hanover, Germany. We signed up for the youth assembly there, for a week with the student Christian group at Goettingen University, and for a week in Berlin with students from East Germany and other countries. We had paid in advance for those weeks and for round-trip passage across the Atlantic on an old troop ship that was now used for students traveling abroad. Beyond that, I had $93 in my pocket to last me for the summer, and Paul had only a few dollars more. I am amazed now that we tried such a thing. We usually stayed at youth hostels, where barracks-type lodging and breakfast could be had during those postwar years in Europe for prices that ranged from about eleven to twenty-five cents in U.S. money. On the road we ate sparingly, never at restaurants. Of course, we also lost weight and found ourselves staring enviously into bakery windows. We stayed with relatives of Jersild on a Danish farm and with a host family in Hanover. That helped.

We saw the Alps, the White Cliffs of Dover, and some of Europe's great cities, including London, Geneva, and Paris. We saw magnificent churches such as the Canterbury Cathedral and St. Peter's, Cambridge and Oxford universities, Michelangelo's *David* in Florence, and the ancient ruins of Rome. We also witnessed some of the terrible devastation of the war, especially in Germany—rubble everywhere in the cities, except for Goettingen, a thousand-years old and virtually untouched by bombs, its charm totally intact. From Munich we took a train to the nearby Dachau concentration camp where horrors beyond horror had occurred. "Here lie the ashes of ten-thousand dead," said one monument outside the ovens that turned humans into dust. "To honor the dead and to admonish the living," read a sign at the entrance. Indeed.

Our German was so rudimentary that we could use only some basic sentences and phrases. Adults often wearied of trying to converse with us, but children enjoyed talking to us as we stood thumbing for rides. We could understand them more easily, and they in turn patiently tried to decipher and sometime giggle at our German.

The highlight of the summer was the Lutheran World Federation assembly, along with our week in Berlin. We were able to attend a few sessions of the main assembly, though I found them a little boring. But the youth section, comprised mostly of students, had lively discussions. We based our Bible study on Paul's Letter to the Philippians, which became a favorite of mine as I read and reread it throughout the summer. Duane Mehl, a seminary classmate, also attended, and we made contact with a handful of Missouri Synod leaders who were there as observers but not members of the Lutheran World Federation because Synod teaches that, by refusing to worship with most of the world's Lutherans, it makes a bold and faithful witness to the purity of its doctrine. Instead it made us look closed-minded, coming from a position of weakness rather than strength. I found it exhilarating to be with other Christians, and to see and hear leaders such as Bishop Hans Lilje, whose witness and suffering during the Third Reich gave him a credibility that stirred me deeply.

I had the same feeling when several dozen of us from the Federation's youth assembly met in Berlin with Christian students from East Germany. They gave me my first direct contact with people who were being persecuted for their faith, paying dearly for it, but giving faithful witness while disavowing any mention of hero- ism. One could only feel a strong, warm bond with such Christians. While in Berlin, we had a communion service in the village of Dahlem, in the church which Martin Niemoeller served when the Nazis came to power and where he spoke against the regime until imprisoned. This experience underscored for me the folly of my church's practice of prohibiting communion with non–Missouri Synod Lutherans (much less non-Lutherans) who don't toe Synod's doctrinal line in every respect. Here were brothers and sisters reflecting the heart of Christ through their suffering and persever- ance, longing for communion with us and we with them. I thought, am I supposed to remain aloof and watch? Where is the Gospel in that? Of course, even the Missouri Synod allows exceptions under emergency circumstances, such as chaplains in combat, and a case could be made that this was such an emergency. But does not life itself and the struggle of faith in the world place every Christian, always, in an ongoing emergency? Is it not complacency and pride to think otherwise? And why would communing with these Christians compromise my faith or diminish my witness? These were thoughts that ran through my mind as we shared the Bread of Life and drank from the Cup of Blessing.

3

Theology and Politics

The class of seminarians to which I belonged initially numbered 200, of which about 160 graduated. In 1951, when other young men our age were being drafted to fight in Korea, we started seminary, a privilege that I, at least, did not sufficiently appreciate until I learned that my friend Dave Becker had been near-fatally riddled with bullets and shrapnel in the battle of Heartbreak Ridge. We seminarians were a fascinating collection of wannabe pastors. I've long thought that writing a book about our class would be a worthy project. If it were ever done, the real heroes should be those who worked faithfully through the years without fanfare or expectation of acclaim, preaching and living the Gospel, making no small sacrifices along the way and doing it all for the love of Jesus and people.

Still, some in the class stood out, or surprised us by standing out later. Perhaps the brightest among us was Paul Heyne. Paul won the American Legion's national oratory contest when he was a senior in high school. He became a prominent economist, and after the collapse of the Soviet Union, spent much of his time in Eastern Europe helping countries move toward a free-market economy. It wasn't what any of us had in mind at Concordia, but he certainly distinguished himself in service. Paul died at the age of sixty-eight of pancreatic cancer.

Ralph Bohlmann, soft-spoken and scholarly, became a professor of systematic theology at Concordia Seminary, St. Louis, where he was among five conservatives on the faculty who refused to protest an attempt by Synod president Jacob Preuss to remove the seminary's president, John Tietjen, and other faculty members. Ralph became the next president of that much-diminished seminary, and a decade or so later president of the Missouri Synod. Though

25

elected as a conservative, Ralph was so vilified by hard-core conservatives that he gradually shifted to more moderate views.

Paul Erdman dropped out after his third year at the seminary and later became president of an American bank in Switzerland. He wrote a string of bestselling novels, the first of which, *The Billion Dollar Sure Thing*, was the story of an international banker who gets involved in a fraudulent scheme to make a fortune. It was reported to be somewhat autobiographical, because his involvement in speculative investments had landed him in a Swiss prison, where he started writing. I had no clue of his writing talents, but another classmate, John Ellwanger, apparently did. In class one day Paul drafted a letter to the actress Debbie Reynolds, who was in St. Louis starring in a stage play, asking her for a date. He gave the letter to John, who signed and mailed it. A few days later Debbie Reynolds called John's dorm and invited him to a performance and a backstage introduction. Such are the breaks in life!

Sam Hoard's extra internship kept him from graduating with my class, but we still claim him. Sam was the only African American in the entire seminary those years. We had a separate seminary in Greensboro, North Carolina, for training black clergy; with rare exceptions, ministry among black people was segregated. The civil rights movement was just beginning to emerge. So Sam's presence at the seminary served as an enormously important reminder of what kind of church we needed to become. He also kept the issue of race alive in conversation. He had learned German in prep school and knew it well enough to preach it— which was more than most seminarians could say. Some of Sam's best stories had to do with the reaction of people who had invited him to preach in a German service and their astonishment when he arrived. On one occasion, his district convention was debating the issue of segregation in the church. A crusty pastor warned that integration could lead to intermarriage. "Would you want to marry a Negro?" he asked. Sam stepped to the mike and said, "Well, I married one, and I think she is pretty nice!" The laughter that followed put things in perspective. Sam had that gift.

There were many others in the class whose achievements became known. Mark Herbener served as a bishop in the Evangelical Lutheran Church in America, and Roy Maack as a Missouri Synod district president (the equivalent of bishop). Ray Martens became a college president. Others taught or served in specialized fields, including a number of seminary or university professors. But, as I say, the real stars were the unsung faithful who neither sought nor achieved much recognition.

Interest in the ecumenical movement grew on campus during my years there, but it was mostly talk. The student body's membership in the Association of Lutheran Seminarians was dropped my first year, on orders from Synod's board of directors or the seminary's board. That did not please me. I understood, however, that Missouri Synod efforts to reach across denominational lines, even to other Lutheran church bodies, required walking on eggs. In 1945 a statement by forty-four prominent Missouri Synod pastors and theologians questioned Synod's policy of prohibiting altar, prayer, and pulpit fellowship with those not in complete doctrinal agreement with Synod. The statement said the policy was based on an erroneous understanding of Romans 16:17 ("Mark them which cause divisions and offenses contrary to the doctrine which ye have learned; and avoid them;" which we had memorized in confirmation class from the King James version). The signers called for discussion and reconsideration of this position. Instead, the statement became a lightning rod for ultraconservatives, who rang an alarm, charged the signers with heresy, and threatened to run them out of the Church. Sensing that fear was obscuring reason, and concerned that the Synod might be torn apart, the signers agreed to withdraw their statement from public consideration. From this, many seminary professors and others learned to walk on eggs.

When my father attended Concordia Seminary in the 1920s, he and a few other students went to hear the evangelist Billy Sunday— as observers. They were told not to join in worship. Billy Sunday said, "All who believe in Jesus, stand up!" Not wanting to participate, the students stayed in their seats while everyone around them stood. "What kind of witness did we give?" Dad asked in exasperation years later. "By sitting we told people we didn't believe in Jesus."

Like students today, we had less to risk and were more impatient than our professors. Although talk of unity across denominational lines seldom went further than talk, six of us arranged days of exchange with six students from Augustana Lutheran Seminary in Rock Island, Illinois (affiliated at the time with a Lutheran body of

Swedish origin). We visited their classes for a day, and they came to St. Louis and sat in on ours for a day. We were impressed. They were impressed. On another occasion I invited Herluf Jensen, president of the Lutheran Students Association, to come and speak to a small number of us informally. I can't point to any results of these modest efforts, but I believe seeds were sown that have born fruit in ways that cannot be traced. That's how growth usually takes place. In these and other ways we were beginning to ask questions and hoped that the Missouri Synod would become less aloof, less legalistic, and more genuinely Christian.

Encountering Corruption

In late 1953, during my third year at the seminary, my brother Paul decided to run for the Illinois state legislature and got me involved in his campaign. Over the previous five-and-a-half years, Paul had put the newspaper on a solid financial footing and helped to bring about a number of improvements in Troy by highlighting such things as the need for a sewer system and a library.

He had also butted heads with Madison County's corrupt political establishment. Sitting in a little Troy diner for lunch, he noticed some punchboards, which gave customers a chance to win up to $5 for a 10 or 25¢ punch. The proprietor complained to him that he had to buy the punchboards from the right man, otherwise one of the sheriff's deputies would come in and tell him his punchboards were illegal and make him pay $30. Paul found that there were thirteen places in Troy with punchboards, and he was able to confirm the same connection with the sheriff's office. That began a long and complicated look into suspicious law-enforcement practices, including those for prostitution houses and large gambling casinos in the county, all illegal, but all tolerated by the Madison County sheriff and its state's attorney (usually called the district attorney in other places). Because Madison County is located across the Mississippi River from St. Louis, its vices could draw from a fairly large population.

Paul began to publish documentation of these illegal operations, as well as the complicity of Sheriff Dallas Harrel and State's

Attorney Austin Lewis in failing to enforce the law. The front page of *The Troy Tribune* often gave detailed descriptions, along with editorials demanding action. But either no action or only token action was forthcoming. Paul met with Governor Adlai E. Stevenson and urged him to have the state close these facilities in view of the breakdown of local law enforcement. One day Paul received a letter from Stevenson's office assuring him that action would be taken. So his newspaper's next headline read: "Big County Gambling Places to Be Closed." When the paper arrived at Musso's restaurant, a popular spot among officials in the country seat of Edwardsville, someone held up the paper and said, "Did you see what Simon had to say this week?" The place rocked with laughter. Three hours later fifty-one state police swooped into the two largest casinos for the first such state-police raid in Illinois history. The raid, featured in *Life* magazine, included the arrest of fifty-four men and the release of approximately a thousand customers.

Paul subsequently pressed charges against the sheriff before a grand jury and asked the Illinois Bar Association to disbar the state's attorney. Both efforts fell short, but were well covered in the media, which put additional pressure on officials to enforce the law. Madison County continued to have enforcement problems, but not on the same scale, and it gradually became a much cleaner county.

While this was going on, Paul took me to a dinner to hear Gov. Stevenson address the county bar association. Stevenson scolded the lawyers for allowing corruption in the county. They did not applaud. At a reception afterward, Paul introduced me to Austin Lewis, the state's attorney he was trying to get disbarred. I pictured Lewis with horns and my heart began to pound, but I was astonished at how friendly Paul was with him. They chatted like old neighbors. By distinguishing between sin and sinner, Paul's theology and practice were obviously better than mine.

At about this time, Senator Estes Kefauver of Tennessee, who headed the Senate Crime Investigation Committee, held hearings in St. Louis. Paul was called as a witness, and his testimony was broadcast over St. Louis–area television. *Newsweek* printed an article about Paul with his picture, which made him a bit of a local legend. But with the Korean War on, Paul, then twenty-two, joined the Army, was assigned to the Counter Intelligence Corps and placed in Coburg,

Germany, along the Iron Curtain that divided Communist Eastern Europe from the West. Paul Jersild and I visited him there while hitchhiking in Europe, and toured the Coburg castle, where Martin Luther lived in hiding for six months during 1530. The three of us also saw a Wagner opera at nearby Bayreuth—a bit heavy for my taste, but as they say, his music isn't as bad as it sounds.

After serving two years, Paul returned to Troy. Ray Johnsen had taken charge of the newspaper during those years and continued doing so. This gave Paul the opportunity to challenge the Madison County political establishment. He decided to run for the state legislature. I spent most of my Christmas break in 1953 with Paul as he met key Democrats prior to his announcement. One evening he discussed strategy with Alan Dixon, the youngest member of the Illinois House of Representatives at the time, who came from a district just south of Madison County. None of us could have guessed that the two of them would one day occupy both Illinois seats in the U.S. Senate. Paul made personal visits to key party leaders, including every precinct committeeman (and they were all men). But first he went to the home of the party chairman, Kenny Ogle. Ogle was a friendly, obese, cigar-chomping man. We sat around a table in his kitchen when Paul told him he intended to run for state representative.

"Do you have money?" Ogle asked.

"No," Paul replied.

"Do you have an organization?"

"No."

"Then take my advice, Paul, and don't do it. You'll just get hurt."

So it went, one committeeman after another. Not much encouragement. But Paul had a way of letting people know he respected them and considered them friends, even if they couldn't support him. He knew that party leaders would supply the committeemen with money, much of it tied to gambling operations, which would require precinct workers to support his opponents. That would pay for many drivers, many workers, and a well-proven network for delivering votes. The evening after Paul announced his candidacy, the Democratic executive committee met and unanimously voted to oppose him.

Paul's slender hope depended upon two things. First, in the primary election each party in each district nominated two candidates for state representative, and in the November election three of the four would be elected. So Paul could come in second in the primary contest and still be nominated. Second, voters normally voted for two candidates. But if someone voted only for one, that candidate would receive two votes. So Paul encouraged people to vote only for him in that race. However, both of Paul's opponents were entrenched and well-liked incumbents.

Using folders that contained endorsements of newspapers and reminders of his record in fighting the corrupt Madison County machine, Paul went out to meet as many voters as possible. He was good at it. He worked his way through business districts, restaurants, and bowling alleys—almost any place where people gathered. He went door-to-door in the daytime and attended public meetings in the evening, always "working the crowd" with handshakes and invitations to vote for him. Mom phoned so many people in different towns that one of the party leaders asked, "How many mothers does Simon have?"

Paul also got volunteers to go door-to-door. At the seminary I did door-to-door work in the dormitories, lining up carloads of students to go across the river on Saturdays. Dozens of them did so. Given the disposition in the Missouri Synod to stay out of politics, I think this experience convinced many future pastors and leaders that public service can be an important way of helping people. I still meet old friends from the seminary who recall with satisfaction the role they played in this campaign.

By the time the primary election came, we had covered just about every house in the district. The response of people encouraged us to think that Paul had a shot at being nominated. A number of newspapers, including *The St. Louis Post-Dispatch*, endorsed Paul editorially, while acknowledging that he had little chance of winning.

Then came election day. Polls opened at 6:00 a.m., as I recall, and the dozen or so of us who were available that day fanned out to cover different towns with last-minute efforts. But what we saw shattered our hopes. Everywhere, it seemed, especially in some of the poorest and most densely populated areas, the streets were alive. At six o'clock in the morning! Cars by the dozens were driving people to the polls. Workers swarmed like flies, all carrying stacks of sample ballots marked for Paul's opponents. I ran into people who had promised to support Paul and who now greeted me like an old friend—but they too were carrying sample ballots marked for his opponents. I was especially dismayed by heavy activity in poor black neighborhoods. Some of the election workers there knew of Paul's stand against discrimination and his membership in the National Association for the Advancement of Colored People. People there were being ill-served by the political establishment, but evidently too poor to turn down money from it on election day. I felt betrayed. We went home that evening discouraged and told our parents that Paul had lost. The machine had overwhelmed us. Paul had reserved Troy's humble town hall that evening for people who wanted to join us in hearing the returns. We no longer looked forward to that.

Then it happened. Precinct after precinct called in, and to our amazement Paul was running way ahead in almost every case, even in areas where the machine was most dominant. Precinct committeemen and others came dropping in unexpectedly to offer their congratulations and soon the hall was crowded with well-wishers. A lot of the organization's paid workers, it turned out, were carrying Paul's voters to the polls, and evidently many who carried ballots for his opponents conveyed their personal preference for Paul. *The St. Louis Globe-Democrat* had Paul's picture on the front page the next day with a story headlined, "Nomination of 25-Year-Old Publisher Stuns Old-Timers." With more than 30,000 votes, Paul ran almost 10,000 ahead of his nearest opponent. We could hardly believe it.

4

Pastoral Formation

In the spring of 1954 all third-year seminarians were assigned intern-ships ("vicarages") for the coming year. I was happy to be placed at St. Matthew's Lutheran Church in New York City. The church was char-tered in 1664 after the British seized New Amsterdam and renamed it New York, and when I arrived the church office still held records going back to 1706, signed by Pastor Justus Falckner. The church had changed location a number of times, and had fled Harlem to avoid racial integration, but by 1954 it was a thriving, inclusive congregation in Inwood, a densely populated neighborhood of low- and middle-income residents on the northern tip of Manhattan.

St. Matthew's was considered by many seminarians to be the pick of the crop, partly because of its location, but even more because of its pastor, Alfred W. Trinklein, and the diversity of the neighborhood and church. Trinklein excelled as a warm, wise, and faithful guide to fledg-ling seminarians. One of the perks of this particular internship was the chance to be a frequent guest in his home and in that of Oswald C. J. Hoffmann. "Ossie," as he was affectionately called, was the widely known public relations director of the Missouri Synod. He and his family belonged to St. Matthew's where, as the nominal assistant pas-tor, he preached once a month, as I did also. During my year there, Hoffmann became speaker for the *Lutheran Hour*, an international radio broadcast. He was a great preacher and a wonderful Christian, with a twinkle in his eye and a contagious belly laugh. He remained actively engaged in preaching until his body quit at the age of ninety-three. Until the very end he carried his Greek New Testament into the pulpit for sermons and translated directly from it.

During my first week at St. Matthew's, Pastor Trinklein took me with him on home visits and hospital calls, then handed me a full platter of assignments. These included seeing prospects and shut-ins, canvassing housing projects, preaching once a month, teaching the seventh grade preconfirmation class, and leading high-school youth activities.

The youth group had gifted members who put on an impressive mission festival for the congregation, as well as a pretty good stage play. We had beach outings, Bible study, and endless informal discussions. Some of us attended a UN roundtable for youth, which helped us think about international affairs as an arena for Christian service. Once we went to the old Polo Grounds ballpark to watch the Brooklyn Dodgers play the New York Giants. I saw Jackie Robinson hit the hardest line drive I've ever seen. With an ear-splitting crack, the ball shot out toward the left-centerfield fence, head-high, faster and farther than I would have thought possible.

For one of the youth group sessions, I invited as a guest speaker Dr. Howard Selsam, director of the Jefferson School of Social Science, the Communist party's instruction center in New York. I had gone there to catch a couple of lectures, partly out of curiosity, but also because I thought Communism to be not only a wrong-headed and dangerous movement, but one that attracted people as an alternative "religion," claiming ultimate truth about history and human society. I wanted our young people to hear it, to understand why—given injustices in our own country—it had such a wide appeal, and to see how false its assumptions are. We heard him respectfully, and I think the session led to a better understanding both of Communism's appeal and of Christian faith. This happened in the era of McCarthyism, and in retrospect I am amazed that no one in the congregation tried to run me out of town.

About the same time I also took a couple of courses at Union Theological Seminary in New York, one on religion and sociology taught by Eduard Heimann, who had fled Germany during the Nazi era, and the other on Christianity and Communism, taught by John Bennett, Searle Bates, and Reinhold Niebuhr, perhaps the most influential Protestant American theologian of the twentieth century. He spoke while sitting in a chair, having had a stroke. But whether lecturing without notes or answering questions, he spoke sentences that invariably seemed camera-ready for print. (Years later, Niebuhr's widow became a generous supporter of Bread for the World, and

John Bennett, also an active member of Bread, suggested some helpful changes on the manuscript of one of my books.) A term paper I wrote for that course became the core of my bachelor of divinity thesis the following year, so I asked for suggestions with that in mind. I got the paper back with an A and useful handwritten comments. To my disappointment it had an illegible signature, obviously that of some graduate assistant, so I noted the comments and threw the paper away. Years later I bought a book on Niebuhr's theology and emblazoned on the cover was that same illegible signature. I had discarded a personal note from Reinhold Niebuhr.

I also spent a day visiting the East Harlem Protestant Parish, which had gained some attention as an inner-city mission started by a few recent Union Seminary graduates while they were still students. That gave me a fascinating glimpse of an alternative to the pattern of churches fleeing the inner city for the suburbs.

Other forays took me to the Lower East Side of Manhattan, an extremely crowded and economically poor section of the city, where a previous intern at St. Matthew, Milton Rudnick, served a small congregation. I also met Roman Catholic layman Art Stabile one night in Times Square, where he was engaged in old-fashioned street debates with non-Christians and had attracted a small crowd. He had started Campaigners for Christ the King, a small hospitality house for students on the Lower East Side. I visited him there, and he took me to the Catholic Worker and to an Eastern-rite Ukrainian church for a festival evening mass.

My year in New York gave me a chance to engage in activities outside my parish, but in fact my time was almost entirely occupied working with the warm and gracious congregation that was St. Matthew's, and getting to know other real or potential saints in the neighborhood. My year in New York was an altogether beneficial experience, one that instilled confidence that God had called me to the pastoral ministry.

The Seminarian

I returned to the seminary for my fourth year and the special challenge of editing *The Seminarian*, our theological students' journal. For this I got the indispensable help of classmate Harold Remus, who later became an editor of books and scholarly journals, director of a university press, and a published scholar in the area of Christian origins and patristics. We decided to reduce the number of issues from nine to four and expand the journal's size to seventy-two pages. We chose Reformation Day, Epiphany, Easter, and Pentecost as seasonal themes. A glance at the articles those years shows a strong church-in-the-world emphasis. We wanted to think of the Gospel in relation to such issues as racial discrimination, poverty, divisions in the church, Christian vocation, and wooden orthodoxy. The most popular articles may have been four "Tapeworm Letters" by a devil written to his nephew Gastrub, who was assigned to undermine seminarians. These letters, chanced upon by classmate David Luecke, would probably have been admired by C. S. Lewis.

Seminarians wrote most of the articles, though bylines included Jaroslav Pelikan, Richard Caemmerer, Søren Kierkegaard, and Martin Luther—the last two without permission. We also published one by Heidelberg theologian Peter Brunner on "Salary and Celibacy," which related to serious discussions some of us were having about celibacy as an option in order to devote one's life more fully to the church's mission.

Our intent with the journal was to tap a wide range of talent and experience by seminary students in ways that might contribute to the growth of spiritual life on campus and beyond, though the main beneficiaries were no doubt the several dozen of us who did the writing. One extended article, "Self-Examination," summarized comments about the seminary's strengths and weaknesses solicited from twenty graduates from Concordia's five most-recent graduating classes. It reflected insights about spiritual formation and studies that would still serve today's students and faculty well.

The most sensitive piece was written by classmate William Jacobsen on "Luther and Orthodoxy." It examined the continuity, as well as differences, between Luther and later Lutheran orthodoxy, one of the roots (along with pietism) from which the Missouri Synod sprang. Jacobsen pointed out that Luther's view of the authority of the Bible had Christ's redeeming work as its central purpose and was the key to its understanding. Subsequent Lutheran orthodoxy, however, based the authority of Scripture upon the inspiration and accuracy of each word in dispensing information on any and every topic. This diminished the centrality of Christ and made faith dependent upon the Bible's inerrancy on all sorts of matters, rather than on the work of Christ. To our chagrin, Jacobsen's article was rejected by a faculty censor. With much effort and the painstaking editorial help of Prof. Paul Bretscher, we were able to move it into print.

Ferment at the Seminary

The reason Jacobsen's article was both sensitive and important lay in the fact that the Missouri Synod has had, from its inception, two main kinds of conservatism. One tends to be rigid and legalistic, allowing not even small departures from a detailed body of doctrine. Hence the furor, mentioned in chapter 1, over the statement of forty-four respected pastors and theologians (such as Ossie Hoffmann) who questioned Synod's stance against pulpit- and altar-fellowship with other Christians. This stream of thought considers the Missouri Synod (and those few others who are in fellowship with it) to be the true visible church on earth. It espouses a form of literalism that insists, for example, that the creation accounts in Genesis be accepted not only as inspired by God for purposes of faith, but also as exact science.

The other stream of thought is more focused on the Gospel of God's love in Christ. It also claims fidelity to the Bible as the word of God, but it maintains that the Bible must be understood according to the purpose for which it was written: to instruct us in faith and life, as it unfolds the account of God's action in history, action that culminated in the life, death, and resurrection of Jesus. According to this thought, the Bible's authority is anchored in the work of Christ for us and for our salvation, and biblical documents should be valued by their role in preparing the way for the coming of Christ or their proclamation of what he has done. Salvation by grace through faith in Christ was the key to the Bible for Luther, and the standard by which biblical writings are to be measured, some more highly than others.

Because watchdog conservatives were eager to alarm both clergy and lay people, moderate conservatives learned to speak with great caution. But during my third, fourth, and graduate years at the seminary, students began to ask for open discussion of these issues and to challenge Synod's rigid view of verbal inspiration and inerrancy. In this way students prompted some faculty members to also enter carefully into the discussion. It seemed to me a healthy development, one that encouraged a living faith grounded primarily not in truth as a collection of accurate statements, but in the person and work of Jesus who *is* the truth.

These discussions generated heat as well as light, especially among a handful of students, who made it their business to find heresy among other students and among faculty members they believed to be departing from authentic Lutheranism. The most determined of these was a student whose family belonged to St. Matthew's Church of my internship. I liked his family a lot and still think of him as a friend. But he seemed driven by the conviction that God had called him to judge the orthodoxy of others and denounce offenders. He did this so recklessly that even the Missouri Synod has refused, to this day, to authorize his ordination. During my postgraduate year at the seminary, several students in his circle made formal charges to the faculty against me and a few others regarding the nature of the authority of the Bible. We had a wide-ranging discussion with a faculty committee appointed to investigate the matter. The charges were ill-informed and the committee gave us a clean bill of health.

I attribute my staying for a postgraduate year to Won Yong Ji, a remarkable Korean who was working on his doctoral degree. Won Yong had fled North Korea during the war and was befriended by a Lutheran chaplain. This began a long journey that led him to Concordia Seminary and instilled in him a determination to plant the Lutheran Church in Korea, which had no permanent presence there. Won Yong persuaded me to become part of the first team of Lutheran missionaries scheduled to begin work in 1958. Since I was in the class of 1956, that raised the question of what to do in the meantime. He urged me to stay another year and get a graduate degree, and I did so, not because I was eager to do graduate work, but because the idea of being part of an innovative new mission appealed to me. So I studied another year, fully expecting to spend the rest of my life in Korea.

God apparently had other plans. In the spring of 1957, shortly before new assignments were issued, Synod's mission board adopted the policy of sending only married students abroad. I wasn't swift enough to comply, so I awaited a different future. Meanwhile Won Yong asked me to be best man in his wedding to Aei Kyong, and I am happy to say that the Lutheran Church in Korea has done very well without me. It is now an outstanding example of effective mission work that has led to a truly indigenous church, and Dr. Ji is an internationally respected figure. One of the original missionaries was my roommate Maynard Dorow, who helped found, taught at, and eventually retired as president of Luther Theological University (and Seminary) near Seoul. Paul Bartling, another classmate, also joined the original team. Paul's father, Victor Bartling, was one of my New Testament professors, and a very good one.

Concordia Teachers College

Though the mission board's policy on marriage came as a disappointment, I was willing to go anywhere and felt at ease. Before many days Dean Leonard Wuerffel asked if I would be willing to take a two-year instructorship in religion at Concordia Teachers College (now Concordia University) in River Forest. Located in an upscale suburb west of Chicago, the college prepared teachers for the Missouri Synod's network of parochial schools. Teaching had never occurred to me, so the invitation came as a surprise. However, I thought that I and perhaps even the students might survive two years of it. The assessment was about right. I am not a scholar and felt unprepared for teaching theology at the college level. I figured it would be good experience, and it did prove useful to me. But the students deserved better.

I taught mainly introduction to Christian doctrine, or "Doc 1" as we called it. The college's required text was Alfred Koehler's *A Summary of Christian Doctrine*. That posed a problem. It summarized Franz Pieper's *Christian Dogmatics*, a 3-volume summary of seventeenth-century Lutheran orthodoxy, and was largely detached from issues and problems of mid-twentieth-century America that I thought Christians should address. So I announced to the class that although Koehler was the official text, I would assume their reading of it, and therefore we would not be dealing with it in class. That gave me the opportunity to present my own lectures—hardly gems of wisdom, and with too much lecturing, but at least they were somewhat connected to life. The course also introduced students to C. S. Lewis's *Mere Christianity* and a few other contemporary writings.

The most rewarding part of those two years was associating with other young faculty members, and most of all those students who excelled, or whose eyes would occasionally let me know that something I had said prompted a light to go on in their minds. I wanted to convey faith in Christ as a living, life-encompassing reality. But I wish I could have done it better.

While at Concordia Teachers College, I learned that Prof. Martin Scharlemann would be guest lecturer at Synod's Northern Illinois district convention. Scharlemann had been one of my New Testament professors and had served on the faculty committee that heard charges against a few of us. Afterward he had sent a personal letter to each of us saying that he wanted to put in writing his opinion that the charges were baseless and that he would vouch for our theological integrity. Not long after, Scharlemann decided to go public in urging a more evangelical view of scriptural authority. A retired military chaplain who had achieved the rank of brigadier general, Scharlemann exuded an authoritarian style. He tended to be not only bold, but commanding, and he brought this trait into a highly charged theological controversy.

I arrived at the convention in time to hear him reply to comments from the floor which, not surprisingly, were hostile. But his responses alarmed me. He berated his detractors, telling them they didn't know what they were talking about and had better go home and study. He tried to squelch views that were deeply felt and deserved a respectful hearing. He was waving a torch at kerosene, feeding the flames of opposition, assuring that his views would *not* be considered. He gave similar presentations at other district conventions, became so controversial that he withdrew his papers with an apology, and eventually reverted to the position he had been criticizing. In this process he played an instrumental role in polarizing our church body. Instead of inviting people to thoughtful reflection, he had sowed seeds of division.

This poisoned atmosphere eventually allowed rigid conservatives to seize control of the Missouri Synod in 1969, electing as president Jacob Preus, who sought the ouster of key professors at Concordia Seminary. This triggered a walkout of 90 percent of the seminary faculty and students in protest, and the launching in 1974 of Christ Seminary, popularly called Seminex (Seminary in Exile). Concordia was left a shell of its former self and the Missouri Synod was soon bereft of some of its most able and devoted servants, including many of my classmates.

Denver

After two years of teaching I received a call to serve as assistant pastor of St. John's Lutheran Church, a large congregation near downtown Denver, where I was ordained and installed on September 13, 1959. The pastor, Paul Hansen, had achieved prominence as a family life specialist. I found him to be an excellent pastoral leader, and the two of us got along well. I enjoyed working with him and the congregation, not least because it had a large contingent of young adults, many of whom had streamed into Denver from Iowa, Nebraska, and other states to begin careers away from home. In addition, I lived with Ed and Norma Boehne and their three young children. Ed taught seventh grade at the church's parochial school, and the Boehne's treated me like a member of the family, which added immeasurably to my enjoyment of living in Denver.

Denver—the city, its people, the mountains just a few miles west, the weather—I loved all of it. Denver had not yet developed a bad case of smog. And I thoroughly enjoyed the congregation, which was growing but constantly changing as people moved in and out of Denver. Paul Hansen was a workhorse who set a fast pace for me, but he was very personable. I didn't sufficiently realize at the time how blessed I was to have had such good pastoral mentors, first my internship and then as Paul's assistant. Good mentors, easy to get along with, are gifts not to be taken for granted.

As I had imagined my adult life unfolding in Korea, so now I imagined myself serving in Denver far into the future. When I received an official call to be pastor of a church in Tulsa, Oklahoma, I turned it down with little hesitation.

Then I received a similar call from Trinity Lutheran Church in Manhattan, New York, the same congregation on the Lower East Side that I had visited a couple of times while interning in that city. Trinity was an exceptional situation: the "most inner" of inner-city challenges. This caused me great discomfort, because I did not want to leave Denver or St. John's, yet Trinity represented the kind of place that I had faulted the church for neglecting. Among those I sounded out for advice was Erv Prange, pastor of St. Mark's Lutheran Church in Brooklyn's Bushwick section, another inner-city parish. I knew Erv from the seminary, where as a war veteran he had a few years and a lot of experience over the rest of us. Never one to withhold an opinion, Erv wrote, "Look, Art, guys are lining up to take your place in Denver. But nobody is willing to come to the Lower East Side." I knew he was right. So I thanked the congregation and Pastor Hansen profusely for their exceptional friendship and added the following in my farewell sermon:

> Trinity compels me to come because it presents a most unique mission challenge. The people who live in this famous tenement district are often God's forgotten people, abandoned by Christians who have fled to the suburbs. I accept the call knowing that there are many who are able and willing to do the urgent work that would be mine at St. John's, but few who are in a position to face the less pleasant side of crowds and slums in the concrete jungles of New York....I will leave with the knowledge that in Christ we have a future together, for in Him we seek an eternal city whose maker and builder is God.

5

New York's Lower East Side

On Good Shepherd Sunday, April 16, 1961, twelve hours before the nation launched its disastrous Bay of Pigs invasion of Cuba, I was installed as pastor of Trinity Lutheran Church, East Ninth Street and Avenue B, on Manhattan's Lower East Side.

"It's like stepping into another world!" my brother Paul said, seeing old five-story tenements lined up wall-to-wall along the street and smack up against the sidewalk. Disheveled kids, old cars, and battered garbage cans gave added indications of poverty. The precinct in which the church stood occupies less than one square mile, but contained more than a hundred-thousand residents. Many came from earlier waves of immigrants who had landed at Ellis Island and settled in ethnic enclaves. They found cheap housing in these nineteenth-century tenements, which were built specifically for poor people. They formed Jewish, German, Irish, Italian, Ukrainian, and Polish clusters, among others, along with more recent African American arrivals from the South and a growing influx of Puerto Ricans. Most of the children in my part of this precinct came from black and Puerto Rican families. Two avenues away, along the East River, low-income public-housing projects towered above the tenements. (Tenements, by the way, have been home to more Americans over the years than log cabins or farm houses.)

My new flock consisted of a few dozen faithful old-timers from what had been, until 1939, a German-speaking congregation, plus a handful of newer members. I came as a pastor, not a social worker, and my job was to share the Gospel in word and sacrament. I knew that fostering growth in the congregation meant getting acquainted in the neighborhood and visiting people in their apartments. Crime, substance abuse, broken homes, single parents, school dropouts, and

43

empty refrigerators were commonplace. I was struck by the contradiction between high unemployment and solvable problems existing side by side. Why couldn't we train and hire people to repair housing or tutor children who lagged in school? Why not solve one problem (unemployment) by solving another (illiterate kids)? We are not always good at using our most valuable resources (people) to improve the quality of life, with the result that problems get worse, to the detriment of all. These thoughts came to me as I carried the Gospel from home to home and wondered how we could more effectively reflect God's love.

As a mission congregation, Trinity had the advantage of support from the Atlantic District of the Missouri Synod. That enabled us to have a full-time lay assistant in Ted Prueter, a former school teacher, who had responsibility for work with children and who also made home visits. Ted, Elaine, and their infant son were living in cramped quarters near the church, while the pastor's residence was a spacious apartment north of the neighborhood in all-white, middle-income Stuyvesant Town. I insisted that we trade quarters, because the Preuters needed the space, and I felt the need to identify fully with people in the neighborhood by living with them and not above them. I use the term *neighborhood* and Lower East Side almost interchangeably, but in fact neighborhoods there often change from one block to another.

By now you are probably thinking, "It must have been hard to live there"—and it was for those who felt trapped and wanted out. That was the case for most of our young people. In exchanges we had with suburban counterparts, our teenagers could be scathingly critical of the neighborhood. I think it was their way of saying, "Don't identify me with what you see here. I'm better than that." One of them read a poem he had written entitled "The Agony of the Lower East Side and the Ecstasy of Moving Out."

Along with its problems, however, the area had a fascinating side as well. Things were always happening—not always good things, but you never worried about being bored. We had endless variety and creative people. I think of Nicholas, the old Russian scientist who had achieved some distinction in the Soviet Union, but fled for his life, and now sold newspapers at a little storefront on Avenue B.

Nick always offered thoughtful conversation when I bought my *New York Times* each morning.

Despite its poverty, the Lower East side is said to have produced America's only intellectual working class, largely because of Jewish immigrants. It had been a hotbed of activity: organizing for causes and debating ideas. It played a significant role in the labor movement and spawned many high achievers, including baseball great Hank Greenberg, composers Irving Berlin and George Gershwin, and senators Jacob Javits and Daniel Patrick Moynihan. Harry Hopkins, President Roosevelt's most trusted advisor, began his professional career as a social worker at the Christadora settlement house across the street from our church, though abandoned during my time. Years later I was riding from an Iowa airport for a joint speaking engagement with sociologist Daniel Bell, who told me that he had grown up on Szold Place, a couple of blocks from the church, and had attended the public elementary school opposite our parish house.

I am barely skimming the surface. There was Ed Marshall, an authentic beatnik of devout faith. He pulled a dozen of his mostly secular cohorts, together with our staff, in the church basement for free-ranging discussion that included drug users, a few Christian charismatics, a couple of professional actors, and Peter Orlovsky, companion of poet Allen Ginsberg. I was struck by the ability of drugs to produce squishy thinking. Yet in this little marketplace of competing hopes the Gospel also got a hearing.

Other local attractions included Pat Maloney, an intense and unconventional Irish-born priest and the founder of Lazarus House for troubled teenage boys, just two tenements from our parish house. Mobilization for Youth, one of the more prominent experiments of the War on Poverty, became a force for change in the neighborhood through community organizing, but it faded away as the war in Vietnam devoured poverty funds. The Lower East Side had a huge influx of hippies in the late 1960s, and with them a spike in drug use and promiscuity, not to mention confrontation with police. They were harbingers of cultural change.

The congregation and the wider network of parishioners occupied most of my time and energy. Our youth group got a tremendous boost from one of our members, George Saunders. An African American, George was an accomplished boxer, gymnast, and jazz buff who excelled in relating to young people. He brought his gymnastic skills to church, taught them to the guys, and gave all of us a model of a Christian life.

Not long after I came to Trinity, I got a call from George, whom I did not know well at the time. He said, "Pastor, there's someone in my building who really needs help. I think you should come over." I did. Marilyn Torres opened the door, a single mother with five little kids running around the apartment. She looked worn-out and bedraggled. The kids looked bedraggled and hyper. I thought to myself, "They are never going to make it." The family joined the church, and over the years Marilyn got off welfare and earned a college degree. She and her two sons and three daughters chose useful careers. But I am pained to say that Celeste, the middle daughter who became a media specialist, was attending a meeting on the 105th floor of one of the World Trade Center towers when they collapsed. I had last seen Celeste at a celebration of Bread for the World's 25th anniversary, held at Trinity Church, where Bread first began.

I worked hard as a pastor, though not always wisely, because I spent too little time in prayer and reflection. What boosted my spirit most was the faith of people, who despite heavy burdens—or maybe because of them—knew that they had already died with Christ and risen with him to a new life. I think of Marjorie Wheeler, who did a great job as a mother of four, despite a difficult marriage and severe arthritis. Or Henry and Arnold Grell, boys who faced all the dangers of their housing project, but persevered faithfully in church and school and beyond. Or the mother of Darnell, whose son overdosed on heroin just when he had a promising scholarship to begin college. Or the family of Nathaniel, a really nice kid who turned to drugs and was shot and killed trying to rob an undercover policeman. In these and other ways, joy and sorrow intermingled.

I recently stumbled across a poem I had written after one of the hospital visits during those years:

> Why does this little girl have to die?
> She's only fourteen
> and there she lies in silence,
> sad eyes and a shapely face,
> showing ugly scars beneath her cap,
> and her frail young body won't move.

She thinks, but she no longer speaks.
She's been through eight months of this, Lord, eight months:
surgery, tubes down her nose, and countless needles.
Silent stares betray a thousand things
she cannot understand or utter.
Her mother has been through it too,
every day at her bedside,
tearing her heart out as life slips away,
knowing that even the doctors don't know
why this is happening.
She tries so hard to hold back tears
and take it in stride.
They wonder if you are really there and care,
and if there is a resurrection.
Tell them, Lord.

Doing More with More

After a year of dogged work, our little congregation was slowly growing, but it became painfully evident that we needed to find ways of being servants of love to more people in the neighborhood. One way we did that was to persuade our Atlantic District to subsidize work among the large and growing numbers of Puerto Ricans in the area. That enabled us to call and secure an associate pastor, John Puelle, who had served five years in Guatemala and had exceptional language skills. His coming in 1964 enabled us to begin Spanish-language services that added importantly to our mission outreach.

Meanwhile, our lay assistant, Ted Prueter, indicated that because of family responsibilities he wanted to return to teaching. I began to wonder how we might multiply our efforts by using his salary in a different way. I wrote a letter to O. P. Kretzmann, revered president of Valparaiso University in Indiana, proposing that Valpo, as it was called, send four volunteers to live and work with children and their families in our parish for a year, and then replace them each subsequent year with new volunteers. To my delight, Kretzmann replied by inviting me to Valpo. I had never met the man, but heard him speak at national youth conventions, where his reassuring voice and probing reflections hushed audiences and seemed to invoke the presence of God. The moment I stepped into his office he introduced me to Walt Reiner, head of the university's Youth Leadership Training Program, who, he said, would take charge of the program, which they intended to expand immediately to include a number of other inner-city churches, as well as Trinity. I was ecstatic.

That launched the Prince of Peace Volunteers, which began at the end of the school year in June of 1963. We got three Valpo students plus one non-Valpo volunteer. We rented tenement apartments for them, and the five of us—later six, with the arrival of John Puelle—had our meals together in the parish house, which made it easy for us to plan and execute our work as a team. Richard Puelle (younger brother of John) and his non-Valpo colleague, Gerry Lohrmann, immediately clashed, but got over it so well that they married two years later and have been a devoted couple ever since. Richard spent his entire career as a math teacher at Seward Park High School on the Lower East Side, and Gerry served many years in the UN-related Lutheran office for world community. Of the other two volunteers, Terry Bernhardt is a health-care analyst in Minnesota, and Mark Birnschein is an electrical engineer in Milwaukee.

These remarkable volunteers, as well as their successors, spent most of their time getting to know the families of children and teenagers, organizing various activities, and helping to staff after-school events and Sunday school. During the program's third year, NBC did a television documentary showing our volunteers playing stickball in the street with neighborhood kids, conversing with them, and teaching, worshiping, and serving as mentors. There's no doubt that the volunteers changed lives (their own, first of all), and drew more people to Christ and to the church.

St. Mark's and St. John, the Evangelist Lutheran Churches in Brooklyn, whose pastors Erv Prange and Richard Neuhaus, were my closest colleagues in ministry, also received volunteers from the onset of the program. That gave all of us additional opportunities to collaborate. The Prince of Peace Volunteers program thrived until about 1968, when the drafting of young men for the Vietnam War shrank it, but it had already spread overseas, was later renamed the Volunteer

Youth Ministry, and now, along with related efforts, sends about fifty recent college graduates abroad each year.

Colleagues

I had known Richard Neuhaus and Erv Prange at Concordia Seminary. Neuhaus was installed as pastor of St. John the Evangelist in Brooklyn the same day and the same hour that I was installed as pastor of Trinity. St. John's, in the Williamsburg section of Brooklyn, was only four subway stations away on the L train, and St. Mark's a few stops further in the Bushwick area. It was easy for us to get together, and we did so frequently. Richard and Erv are cousins, both of them exceptionally bright and purpose-driven. We kept one another posted on developments in our respective parishes, including the volunteer program, and collaborated with others in getting our Atlantic District to start a new inner-city church in the East New York section of Brooklyn.

I had moved to Trinity just as inner-city ministry was beginning to get much higher visibility in church circles. Some of us sensed the need for a small publication that could be circulated among Lutheran inner-city pastors to help keep us informed of developments in various cities and parishes. The editorship fell to me, with John Christ and Harry Fullilove (pastors in the Bronx from other Lutheran bodies) part of a three-man editorial board. Urban ministry executives of the major Lutheran bodies gave us lists of urban pastors, so in April 1964 we launched *Inner City*, an eight-page mimeographed bimonthly newsletter with a circulation of eight hundred. I became an instant expert by virtue of my new title. Of course, my colleagues were not fooled, though I think the publication served a useful purpose for a few years.

Those newsletters did not reveal an abundance of modesty on my part. I thought we knew what was wrong with the church and the nation, and felt it was our job to let everyone know. The first page of the first issue said, "Perhaps never in history has the Lutheran Church been so well equipped in terms of wealth, numbers and skills for so momentous a task, yet so negligent of it." The task we had in mind was to become a living presence of Christ among the urban poor and to more broadly address some of the huge injustices— mainly racial and economic—that afflicted inner-city neighborhoods. We were not wrong in that, but I was more confident of our solutions and the sins of others than I was of my own limitations.

One example: an article in April 1967 reported a struggle to get Eastman Kodak of Rochester, New York, to hire more African Americans. Churches in that city had organized demonstrations and finally got a signed agreement from Kodak, which it renounced a couple of days later as unauthorized. Two church bodies then announced that they would take action against Kodak as stockholders, but the Lutheran Church in America (LCA), which also held stock, backed away from joining them. I reported that its president, Franklin Clark Fry, "was not favorable to such action," and I asked, "whether this is another instance of carrying money in one pocket and convictions in another." I soon got a call from Fry's secretary inviting me to come and meet with him.

Franklin Clark Fry—great churchman, president of the Lutheran World Federation, key figure in both the National and the World Council of Churches, and "Mr. Protestant" on the cover of *Time* magazine. I entered his office expecting a dressing down, but he surprised me with graciousness. He told me the Kodak situation was complicated, and that he agonized over it, wasn't sure of the right thing to do, and welcomed my thoughts. So we talked. I told him why I felt as I did, but admitted that my information left me short of certainty, as well. I don't think our conversation led either of us to a different conclusion, but Fry had given me an example of humility, which I needed, and I left his office with enormous respect for the man.

Vatican II

When Pope John XXIII convened the Second Vatican Council in 1963, he not only opened a window for fresh air in the Roman Catholic Church, but in other church bodies as well. Vatican II had an unexpected impact on our own congregation—first of all, in prompting a careful reexamination of our Sunday liturgy.

It happened this way: St. Brigid's Church, with its sanctuary just a block away from our own, had gotten an experimental pastoral team of three young priests to replace Monsignor Lynch, who had recently died. Monsignor Lynch was pre–Vatican II in outlook and I had little contact with him. His replacements, however, were eager to get acquainted. When we heard that they were implementing some of the Council's reforms, a group of us from Trinity visited a festival liturgy one evening. For the first time we witnessed a Roman Catholic Mass in English, with the priest presiding behind a free-standing altar. The singing was robust, some of it accompanied by guitar. We saw children bringing bread and wine to the altar during the offering, as the congregation sang, "Sons of God, hear his holy word, gather round the table of the Lord." Not exactly a Bach chorale, but we had never imagined so lively a Mass.

This experience touched off visits to other churches (including St. John's in Brooklyn, which had also initiated reforms), and subsequent discussions about ways in which we could enrich Trinity's worship. As a result, we began celebrating communion every Sunday, (not the Synod's usual practice). We also pulled the altar away from the wall, had people kneel around three sides of the altar when communing, hung banners above the pews, introduced more variety in our songs, greeted one another with the peace of Christ, recast the prayers in contemporary language, and printed a service booklet that made the structure of the liturgy and its relation to daily life in our neighborhood visually clear. We also invited members to share out loud their concerns or joys for the prayers of the faithful, a practice that caught on immediately and palpably met an unfulfilled need. These changes made a huge contribution to our life as a worshiping community.

St. Brigid's and Trinity both face Tompkins Square Park, so we initiated the practice of having a joint service of the word in the park on Pentecost, and then marching to our respective sanctuaries for the Eucharist. In this way we celebrated our unity in Christ while acknowledging, with regret, remaining differences that kept us from a full expression of that unity. On another occasion we had a Jesuit priest from nearby Nativity Church talk to the congregation about Vatican II. These were heady days for the budding of unity and I was invited twice to preach at special ecumenical services in Roman Catholic churches.

In one of the more interesting developments these years, Neuhaus hosted monthly dialogues with several Roman Catholic priests from Brooklyn and several Lutheran pastors. I was the learner, seldom the contributor, in these discussions, which informed the mind and nourished the soul. Neuhaus, of course, was way ahead of most of us in his grasp of the theologies of both traditions, and was disposed to clearing the path toward eventual reunion between the churches of Wittenberg and Rome. But I do not think he was yet close to making his eventual journey "home to Rome" as he would later describe his decision to become a Roman Catholic and his ordination as a priest.

6

Poverty and Civil Rights

Three months after moving to New York I was invited to take part in a meeting of community leaders from our section of the Lower East Side, regarding a three-block site near the church that the city had designated as suitable for urban renewal. It contained mostly old commercial shops, a few warehouses, and only 165 tenement apartments. An official of the city's Housing and Redevelopment Board explained that they sought "citizen participation," as required by federal law, and asked for our help in determining what neighborhood people wanted and needed on that site. Only a handful of people showed up for the meeting, and to my surprise, they asked me if I would be willing to head a local citizens' group to respond to the city's request. I felt flattered to have my talents recognized so soon, though in fact others were too busy and I was naïve. Little did I know that the city had already stacked the deck against us and that I was in for a painful lesson about how the balance of power weighs heavily against poor people.

The Tompkins Square Housing Committee formed and began holding public meetings to invite citizen participation. We got volunteers to interview residents on the site and learned that they paid low rents, that about half of them had very low incomes, that about half of the apartments were overcrowded, and that almost three-fourths of the tenants wanted to remain on the site, if they could afford the rents.

Robert Dennis, a member of our committee and a city planner (though not employed by the city), together with another city planner and an architect, formed a team that made a building-by-building inspection not only of the three-block site, but of eight blocks immediately surrounding the site. They found that a few structurally solid buildings needed no repair. A dilapidated few required demolishment within ten years, but the vast majority of them were structurally sound, so repairs could bring them up to building code standards.

Based on this information we sought to avoid wholesale bulldozing in favor of selective preservation of habitable buildings, while tucking in new row houses as needed in "vest pocket" sections. So we proposed—

- That most of the new housing should offer rents that current residents could afford;

- That the city redraw the lines for the proposed site to exclude two clusters of tenements in relatively good shape in order not to further deplete the supply of low-rent housing; and

- That the site not be treated as an isolated area, but as the first of a series of stages to repair and replace housing in the area without displacing large numbers of residents from the neighborhood.

These proposals were developed over many months with input and support of neighborhood people in public meetings, as well as by community groups in the immediate area. But no dialogue with the city's Housing and Redevelopment Board ever materialized. Some of us met with chairman Milton Mollen and a few of his board members. They listened politely, but gave us no clue as to what their planners had in mind. The project-development chief said technicians did not want neighborhood people "peeking over their shoulders." Mollen assured us that as soon as their "preliminary concept" was ready ("the most tentative sort of sketch," he said), we could sit down with them and discuss matters of substance.

Then, without notifying us, on June 20, 1963, Mollen unveiled for the press and public their "tentative final concept," which ignored priorities urged by the community and proposed instead a high-rise, middle-income development. It was classic "urban removal" from the standpoint of low-income people. I found out about the unveiling one day before it occurred only because Murray Illson, a *New York Times* reporter, called to ask if I would be on hand to respond. I couldn't be, but we quickly whipped out a news release that protested the procedure and outlined the community's proposal. One of our members distributed the release as reporters arrived. As a result, Illson's front-page story in the *Times* the next morning featured our challenge as well as the board's plan. Its headline: "Housing Planned at Tompkins Sq: But Minister Charges Setup Means 'Urban Removal' of Slum Residents." Mollen, however, made clear that he wanted to implement the plan as fast as possible. So much for dialogue!

The Manhattan Borough president subsequently paid me a surprise visit at the parish office, but his purpose was to soothe, not listen.

In January at an open meeting in a public school near the site, a public gathering of almost three hundred people—a huge turnout in our neighborhood—heard both plans presented on an equal-time basis. Mollen and staff members presented the Housing and Redevelopment Board's plan. People listened to both proposals and asked questions. Afterward the audience voted almost unanimously in favor of the neighborhood committee's plan with only four opposing votes. Still the board pushed ahead. We sent letters to officials of the federal housing agency to protest the city's disregard for citizen participation. They replied that the mayor's Citizens' Advisory Committee had reviewed and approved the board's concept, thus meeting the legal requirement. The mayor's *what?* We had never heard of such a committee.

In September, the city's powerful Board of Estimate, chaired by Mayor Robert Wagner, held an open hearing prior to making a final decision. The hearing room was jammed, mostly with our supporters, and in a marathon session I gave initial testimony and produced one speaker after another from the neighborhood, including the sister of Jane Jacobs, author of *The Life and Death of the American City*, who also supported us. I was interviewed on local television for Mike Wallace's "Eye on Housing" program. In these and other ways we continued to press our views. In the end, we gained the concession of two hundred moderate income units among the nine hundred apartments, not insignificant but small compared to the outcome we sought. We had fought Goliath, and Goliath won.

Still, we thought we had a sound idea, so we expanded it to include a much larger section of the Lower East Side. With the help of architect Percival Goodman (brother of writer Paul Goodman) and Bob Dennis, we were able to visually display a plan for upgrading the entire area of about sixty blocks in stages, at modest cost, without displacing residents who wanted to stay. We also sought an ethnic and economic mixture. We shopped the idea around and attracted supporters for it. Among those who showed interest was Congressman John Lindsay, who leaned back in his chair and smiled approvingly at us when Dennis mentioned rumors that Lindsay might be interested in running for mayor. And one of the young neighborhood men who actively supported the plan, John Wilson, later went on to become a highly regarded chairman of the Washington, DC city council. We stirred up a lot of interest, but in the end simply lacked the clout to make it happen.

Faces of Poverty

Among the people I got to know well was the Bauer family—Charles and Evelyn and their two children, Charles, Jr., and Jane. Theirs was a tale of riches to rags, and they showed how hard-working white folks can get mired in poverty, just like any other ethnic group. I visited them frequently, sure to be rewarded with riveting accounts of crises encountered and dreams lost. The episodes were always new, yet always the same. I left their apartment one day, thinking to myself, "If only people could hear their story, they would begin to understand how people can get stuck in poverty." Then the idea struck me: Tell their story. Write a book.

That's how *Faces of Poverty** was conceived. I wanted people to see faces—real flesh-and-blood people from my own congregation, not abstract generalities or mind-numbing statistics—when thinking of poverty. I started with the Bauer family. I told how Evelyn and Charles met, married, and worked together during the World War II years, but then how, after the war, physical disability and hardship ate away at their dreams until they had to find quarters on the Lower East Side.

Then I introduced Edna Moore, a single black mother, and her family. I described the struggles of her own childhood in Harlem, the cruelty of racism, and the difficulty of rearing children when there's not enough food. A hard-working, hotel-service employee, Edna later became the godmother of my first son. Her life reflected a

---

*Arthur Simon, *Faces of Poverty* (St. Louis, MO: Concordia Publishing House, 1966).

heroic effort to survive and thrive under conditions more adverse than most of us can imagine.

A chapter on "postgraduate poverty" told stories of three elderly persons. Ernest Kronnenwett was a gentle soul with only one eye, and that one infected from swimming as a youth in the East River. He had worked as a clerk, but now, near eighty, his only income was $40 a month from Social Security. Half of that went for rent, another five for heat and electricity. Too proud to go on welfare, he "lived" on fifty cents a day.

Margaret Cunningham, a wiry wisp of a woman, had more years than pounds. Twice widowed, she worked well into her seventies as a domestic. At age eighty-one her sole source of income was $86 a month from Social Security, from which $40 paid the rent and $14 paid for medicine, leaving her $1 a day for everything else.

Eddie Elliott, an immigrant from England, had worked in soap factories for sixty-three years. Spry at eighty-six, his dismal, barren apartment of two rooms spoke of hardship behind a ready smile. Like the others, his Spartan income barely allowed him enough to eat. But having been robbed three times, he worried mainly about safety. "What if something happens to me?" he asked.

The full story behind these snapshots of people I knew and loved filled the first half of the book and constituted its heart. The second half built on their stories, taking a broader look at poverty. In it I criticized the church's flight from poor and often racially changing urban areas, reflecting a theology of success rather than the theology of the cross. But the chapter that attracted the most attention was one that described in detail my experience, related above in abbreviated form, with the Tompkins Square Housing Committee in its fight with the city over urban renewal. *The Atlantic Monthly* featured it in April 1966 under the title "New Yorkers without a Voice." That prompted a favorable review of the book by Steven Roberts in the *New York Times* and got me on New York City's most popular call-in radio interview program, "Talk of the Town," which allowed me to respond for two hours to callers, some of them angry. My reward was a handwritten note of appreciation a few days later from my former seminary professor, Jaroslav Pelikan, then at Yale, who heard it on his car radio.

The angry callers were mainly residents of Stuyvesant Town, a huge middle-income housing complex immediately above the Lower East Side. I had described it as the kind of class- and race-stratified urban renewal that we wanted to avoid.

Stuyvesant Town was, in fact, the nation's first urban renewal project. It covered a huge eighteen-block area of what had been part of the Lower East Side. Built privately by the Metropolitan Life Insurance Company with state and federal subsidies, immediately after World War II, it was heralded as "a suburb in the city." Stuyvesant Town became the focus of fights against racial discrimination in housing, triggered the first laws against housing discrimination, as well as a court case that went all the way to the U.S. Supreme Court, which declined to review it. The fact that it generated such controversy on so sensitive an issue related to poverty and race prompted me to write a second book, *Stuyvesant Town, USA: Pattern for Two Americas*. The writing of it taught me a lot, as did the earlier book, and put me in touch with a number of civic leaders.

MetLife defended Stuyvesant Town's exclusion of African Americans by arguing that society wasn't ready for integration, and that change should come gradually and voluntarily, but this only insured that change would not occur. When the New York City Council responded by making discrimination in housing illegal, MetLife postponed integration for years by saying that black folks would have to wait in line like everyone else—and there was a long white line. My manuscript documented all of this, and I was sure the ensuing attention would hasten the pace of integration. I sent the manuscript to Harper & Row, was invited to meet with an editor—a good sign—who told me they didn't want to do it as a book, but Cass Canfield, a literary luminary there, had suggested I condense it for an article in *Harper's* magazine. That was a great opportunity to reach a wide public, but fool that I was, I turned it down, certain that a book would accomplish much more. After a few more publishers rejected my manuscript, New York University Press accepted it, sold a small number that got limited attention, and I ate humble pie.

Civil Rights

During the 1960s the civil rights movement brought a number of ugly racial injustices to public view, and moved the nation to act against them. So deeply was prejudice against people of color embedded in our culture, and so rigidly was it enforced by law in the South, that these changes were passionately, even violently resisted. Stuyvesant Town illustrated the "more genteel" Northern version of institutionalized racism. On the Lower East Side, which was a model of integration by comparison, the apartments that we rented on East Ninth Street for our Prince of Peace Volunteers would not always have been available to African Americans. So entangled were we, and still are, in privileges that others are often denied.

Some of us became active in the Lutheran Human Relations Association of New York with the encouragement of Clemonce Sabourin, board president of the national association and pastor of Mt. Zion Lutheran Church in Harlem. Richard Neuhaus agreed to lead the New York chapter for a couple of years, and its activity reached a peak with the March on Washington, August 28, 1963, when five busloads of Lutherans embarked from New York City. Reports that proved totally false of possible violence in the nation's capital discouraged many from joining the march. But the sight of hundreds of buses rolling down Interstate 95 toward Washington at the crack of dawn instilled a sense of excitement that what was about to happen might help rescue the nation from its gravest moral failure. Even more moving to me were black people lined up along the streets of Washington in front of their homes, waving with approval as we rolled by. Tears welled up at this sight, a reminder to me of the suffering that had prompted the march and how much was at stake for the nation.

The march with its numbers, peacefulness, soaring oratory, and celebrities gave viewers across the nation a righteous alternative to the brutality and injustice many had been witnessing for months on their television sets. Martin Luther King's "I Have a Dream" speech touched the heart of the nation. The march produced a surge of goodwill and passage of the 1964 Civil Rights Act, which banned discrimination in education, employment, and public accommodations.

The Rising of Bread for the World

About a year and a half later, on Sunday afternoon, March 7, 1965, hundreds of black citizens marched peacefully across Edmund Pettus bridge in Selma, Alabama, seeking their voting rights. Their aim was to carry the message all the way to the state capitol building in Montgomery. But on the opposite side of the bridge a phalanx of a hundred Alabama State Police stood shoulder to shoulder blocking the highway. Suddenly they turned on the demonstrators with clubs and tear gas, as other policemen on horseback joined in beating the fleeing marchers. Heads were cracked. Television cameras beamed all of this into living rooms across the land, to the horror of the nation.

The next day at about six o'clock in the evening I got a call from Richard Neuhaus asking if my colleague John Puelle and I would fly down in response to Dr. King's appeal for clergy from around the nation to take part in another attempt to march from Selma to Montgomery on Tuesday. This was the first I had heard of the appeal, since I had isolated myself for the day to work on *Faces of Poverty*. A few hours later we were aloft. On the plane, Mike Stein, newsreporter for radio station WNEW in New York, interviewed me. He asked if I was afraid, and I admitted that I was. I can't remember what else I said, but the interview went on the air, and among the listeners was Trinity parishioner George Saunders, who later told me how proud he felt about my going—which alone made the trip worthwhile because it helped to seal our friendship.

Other clergy were on the flight. We got a few hours of sleep in Atlanta, where clergy from other cities were also converging. After reaching Montgomery, we were driven along a back road (for safety) into Selma by Genevieve Anderson, whose family owned a funeral home in Selma. She had been with the ambulance crew that, despite resistance from police, had driven over the bridge to give aid to the injured. We got out in front of a large Methodist church, the site a few days earlier of a funeral for a member who had been bludgeoned to death near Selma.

Now numbering many hundreds, we milled around as additional clergy arrived. I was surprised to find Wilson Baker, Selma's Commissioner of Public Safety, mingling with the crowd. I had a chance to talk with him for a while and it was apparent that he was sympathetic to our cause, in sharp contrast to County Sheriff James Clark, whose deputies had been assaulting black citizens who came to the courthouse to register to vote. Baker kept saying that he could keep peace as long as we stayed within the city limits and away from the courthouse; otherwise the state troopers or the sheriff's posse would take charge. By this time word had gotten around that a federal judge had issued an injunction against the march, and that Martin Luther King was in consultation about this. Baker told me he thought the group should not march, because "I have a lot of respect for a federal court."

We crowded inside Brown Chapel. Among other speakers, we heard John Lewis, leader of the Student Nonviolent Coordinating Committee, head bandaged from being clubbed unconscious on Sunday. At about 1:45 p.m., Dr. King arrived. Everyone stood and applauded, as TV cameras followed him in. He explained why he thought we must march. He said we were not violating the law, because the Constitution guarantees peaceful assembly. He urged anyone not committed to nonviolence to refrain from marching.

The line began to form, four abreast, with Dr. King in front. I was about a block back in a line several blocks long. To my surprise there was no singing, not even much talking, just an eerie quiet. Some white citizens sat on their porches or looked out windows, and a few stood on the opposite sidewalk, as though they had been instructed to say and do nothing. Their faces were not friendly, some clearly hostile. What struck me most, however, was how totally exposed Dr. King was, and how easy it would be for anyone to shoot him. This man has great courage, I thought, but not long to live.

As we marched over the crest of the bridge, we could see the line of shoulder-to-shoulder state policemen blocking the highway on the other side. I confessed to John, a Methodist minister from Chicago who was next to me, that I had a newspaper stuffed in my beret in case I was clubbed. John silently removed his hat and showed me a towel. We marched on for a few minutes, then the line stopped as the voice of Major John Cloud of the state police came over a loudspeaker. Soon Dr. King asked the marchers to kneel and pray, which we did. Then we began marching again, but this time the leaders made a U-turn and led us back across the bridge to the church. It was packed. I sat on the floor, center front, just a few yards away from Dr. King. I was deeply moved as he paid lavish tribute to Joe Ellwanger, my friend from seminary days and a pastor in Birmingham. Joe and his wife Joyce, on the day before Bloody Sunday, had led the first all-white march by southerners for the civil rights of African Americans. Facing taunts and threats, they had walked to the Selma courthouse steps, where Joe read a statement protesting brutality and urging that the voting rights of black citizens be honored. King recounted this, then announced that another protected march from Selma to Montgomery would soon take place on "Freedom Day," cluminating with a mass demonstration in front of the state capitol.

Afterward, as I stood in front of the church waiting for my ride, King got into a car next to me. A group of young girls, maybe eight or nine years old, surrounded him and he gave each a kiss. It was a touching bit of affection that I chose not to interrupt.

A couple of sullen-faced white members of the Student Nonviolent Coordinating Committee approached me and asked me what I thought of the march. I told them I was grateful for the outcome. They, however, expressed anger that King had not waded into the state police line; they considered this a major setback. That was my first exposure to the internal cleavages that King had to deal with, and it increased my respect for him and his ability to take the initiative while showing restraint. It also indicated to me how far out of touch were those people who considered him a radical.

During our Atlanta layover on the way back, we got word that three clergy marchers had been attacked in Selma, and that James Reeb, a Unitarian minister, had a fractured skull and was in critical condition. A few hours later he died. It was a sobering end to an emotional day.

The Selma marches secured passage of monumental legislation in Congress a few months later. Barely a week after Bloody Sunday, President Johnson personally proposed what became the 1965 Voting Rights Act to a joint session of Congress. In a display of rare presidential eloquence, Johnson said, "At times history and fate meet at a single place to shape a turning point in man's unending search for freedom. So it was at Lexington and Concord. So it was at Appomattox. So it was last week in Selma, Alabama." The nation was never the same.

What amazes me as I look back is the freedom I had as a pastor to do the things I describe in this chapter. I am grateful to the congregation I served for giving me that freedom. I report these things because they shed light on the eventual creation of Bread for the World, but I wish to make clear that I did not neglect ordinary, ongoing parish responsibilities: visiting members and prospects, preaching, teaching, and more. These occupied the vast majority of my time. I did not see writing a book or going to Selma as detached from the Gospel of God's love in Christ or from my parish obligations. All were interwoven into one ministry of word and deed.

Back in New York I continued to be active in racial and economic concerns, occasionally joining a demonstration, but choosing with care and never because I thought it was fun. I took my turn for a couple of years chairing New York's Lutheran Human Relations Association, although Christa Ressmeyer-Klein, just graduated from Valparaiso, did most of the work as an exceptionally skilled, full-time, one-person staff. In addition I served on a racial commission convened by Missouri Synod president Oliver Harms on which Chris McNair also served. McNair's daughter Denise was one of the four little black girls killed in the 1963 bombing of the Sixteenth Street Baptist Church in Birmingham—another event that shook and changed the nation.

They were events that shook and changed me as well.

7

Encountering Hunger

Hunger was no stranger to people on the Lower East Side. I frequently visited families who ran out of food before the end of the month. The church helped when we found out, but people were often too proud or ashamed to ask. A nutritional study that included 619 children from six primary schools within walking distance of the church found that 73 percent had inadequate diets. The children got half or less of the recommended daily requirement of vitamins. One out of every six youngsters was judged nutritionally deficient, based on soft muscles, excessive leanness, and prominent abdomens. Ten of the children interviewed said they had eaten no meals on the previous day. These conditions handed children a big obstacle to learning.

It was common knowledge that neighborhood kids often went to school hungry. We found that to be also the case with children who came to our church. As church attendance grew and more Sunday school kids stayed for worship, we faced the problem of restless children causing disturbances. So we started serving pancakes, milk, and orange juice before Sunday school. To our surprise and delight, the children suddenly became more attentive in church.

Sometime during the mid-1960s, the rise in welfare clients forced a cut in benefits, a blow to families already barely getting by. So we started a voluntary income-sharing program in the congregation, with some of the more prosperous members giving a pledged amount each month that was transferred to those in need. More than $500 was transferred each month, and I think people were as heartened by the generosity of others as they were by the assistance itself.

Campaigning

By the spring of 1968, church attendance was up, and we saw indications that the Gospel was touching the hearts of many people. Much of this was due to the Spanish-language ministry of John Puelle, the work of the Prince of Peace Volunteers, and especially the parishioners who let their friends and neighbors know how Christ entered their lives. I had worked hard in the parish for seven years, so I arranged to take a sabbatical without pay. That gave me an opportunity to campaign for my brother Paul, who was running for Lieutenant Governor of Illinois.

By 1968 Paul had served four two-year terms in the Illinois state assembly. After soundly trouncing the Madison County political machine in his first race, he ran the next three times without its opposition. At the end of each legislative session Paul had received the Best Legislator Award from the Independent Voters of Illinois for his initiative in such things as passage of a "right to know" bill requiring that actions and deliberations of governmental bodies be open to the public, his complete disclosure of personal finances each year, his fight for balanced budgets, and his various measures to expand opportunities for the most vulnerable. At a time when teachers were in short supply, Paul learned that some of the most talented teachers could not find placement because they were black, so he secured passage of legislation that required school districts to practice nondiscrimination in hiring in order to get state aid. In these and other ways Paul taught me that you can do a lot of good for a lot of people through government.

He also acquired a remarkable partner by marrying Jeanne Hurley, a fellow state representative. They found much common ground as they worked together on legislative issues. Their family life and public life intertwined closely until Jeanne's death in 2000, and along the way included two children, Martin and Sheila, and four grandchildren—all very special people.

After eight years as a state representative, Paul decided to run for the state senate. Once again he faced a well-financed opponent backed by the central committee of the Madison County Democrats. But he beat them again, this time by a two-to-one margin. During the next six years he often found himself opposing legislation that he believed was tainted by payoffs. In a move that proved to be something of a bombshell, he wrote an article with journalist Al Balk for the September 1964 *Harper's* magazine entitled "The Illinois State Legislature: A Study in Corruption." He described in detail how money changed hands under the table to secure legislation for special interests. This enraged many of his colleagues, some of whom proclaimed him the recipient of the Benedict Arnold Award. Among those unhappy colleagues was Paul Powell, a powerful downstate legislator who subsequently became secretary of state. When he died in office, he was found to have $800,000 stuffed in shoe boxes in his Springfield apartment.

During his fourteen years in the Illinois legislature, Paul wrote a weekly column that ran in newspapers around the state. He gained a reputation for honesty and independence, spoke frequently throughout the state, and lined up the support of downstate Democratic county chairmen for a run against U.S. Senator Everett Dirksen. But downstate did not include Chicago's Cook County chairman Mayor Richard Daley, whose vote counted for more than all the others combined because Cook County delivered two-thirds of the state's Democratic votes in the primary. Daley considered Paul too independent, so he failed to endorse Paul's run for the U.S. Senate. But Daley, respecting Paul and his downstate strength, did propose him as the party's candidate for lieutenant governor.

The first thing I did was write a thirty-two-page booklet that we printed in mass quantity, telling the story of Paul's life and public service. The booklet was widely distributed throughout the state. But my main job was going from town to town, county by county—walking the business districts, meeting people in stores and on the street, introducing myself as Paul's brother, handing them a campaign folder, and inviting them to consider voting for Paul. I met hundreds of people every day this way, and covered most of the towns in every county by the time the November election rolled around.

I say *I* did this. Actually I returned to New York in midsummer to marry Kaiya Schoonmaker, who had joined Trinity Church a few years earlier, and who now began campaigning with me. It was not your typical honeymoon, of course, but what it lacked in quality it had in quantity, because it lasted more than three months. It also doubled our contacts, because Kaiya could work one side of the street while I did the other. Those months before the election we campaigned almost exclusively in Chicago and surrounding suburbs.

The 1968 campaign was wrenched by the assassinations of Martin Luther King and Robert F. Kennedy, two devastating blows to the entire nation. Paul had spoken at the second anniversary of the Montgomery bus boycott and spent two days with King and his family. These deaths stunned all of us. Another wrenching development was the antiwar demonstrations in Chicago at the Democratic National Convention, where excesses by demonstrators were met with a crackdown by the Chicago police that may have cost Hubert Humphrey the presidency. Our work, however, continued, and I felt that we were getting a warm response for Paul.

While in Chicago, I heard people talk about Jesse Jackson and Operation Breadbasket (later Operation Push) and the efforts to bring more blacks into the workforce of companies that lagged in hiring them. Operation Breadbasket held Saturday morning rallies at a Baptist church on the south side of Chicago, so one Saturday I dropped in. They combined action with hymn singing, preaching, and praying: typical of the civil rights movement. It seemed to me they were on to something, and I wondered what I could learn from this.

On Election Day we went to Paul's home in Troy, where we watched the returns in a rented hall that evening. The race was close and not until late in the evening did it become clear that Paul, a Democrat, had been elected with a Republican governor, Richard Oglevy, the only time in Illinois history that such a split outcome occurred. Dad and Mom watched the returns with us, and a couple of months later Dad gave the invocation at the inauguration. We had no idea that he would soon die from acute leukemia, and that I would see him next on his deathbed, a deep personal loss.

Paul was seen as a likely challenger to the governor in four years. Not having a role in the governor's administration, Paul announced that he would act as a state ombudsman to investigate complaints of people regarding the functioning of government. That gave Paul the opportunity to serve in a useful capacity while preparing a run for the governorship. I entertained dreams of what Paul might be able to do as governor to address hunger and poverty at the state level, and perhaps later nationally.

Lent Touches a Nerve

I returned to New York happily married, feeling that the prospect for Paul's political future looked bright, and eager to get back to normal parish life—if anything on the Lower East Side could be considered normal. Our Prince of Peace Volunteer program had shrunk, thanks to the war in Vietnam and the military draft of eligible young men.

Lutherans have a strong tradition of Wednesday evening Lenten services, although in our neighborhood it was not easy to get people out at night in the dark. We decided to begin our Wednesday evenings in the church basement with a discussion featuring a different topic each evening. After a half hour, we had a Lenten worship that related each topic to the suffering and death of Jesus. One of the topics was hunger, and that discussion touched a nerve. Experiences, observations, and ideas came pouring out. Our church always made a good offering each year for Lutheran World Relief, which prompted one mother to say, "Why don't we have an offering of letters to Congressman Farbstein about hunger?" Other suggestions followed. Someone asked, "Why don't we get our whole church body to do some of these things?" Before long we decided to develop our thoughts into a formal resolution that we could propose to the Missouri Synod, which had a national convention scheduled for that summer.

It fell to me to compose a written resolution, which, along with other suggestions, asked that the president of Synod appoint a commission to study the issue and make recommendations. That did two things for me. First, it intensified my interest in hunger, thinking for the first time that maybe our small congregation could have a large impact on our entire church body. Second, it got me involved in extensive discussions with Dr. Martin C. Poch, a former seminary classmate of my father, who had been appointed chairman of a convention committee assigned to handle proposals about social concerns. As an Army chaplain, Dr. Poch had served briefly at different times under General George C. Marshall (for whom he had great respect) and General Douglas MacArthur (who struck him as arrogant). He could rivet anyone's attention with his World War II experiences. We got to know one another well, and he helped develop a strategy for gaining a favorable hearing for our resolution. The committee and the convention approved our resolution in a somewhat watered-down form, but it included a presidential commission on hunger, which Poch was asked to chair. Our church body's new president, Jacob Preus, did not appoint me to the commission, but Poch later asked him to add me, and he did.

Meanwhile, I picked up a few books to become more conversant with global hunger, about which I knew relatively little. Some of the books, such as Paul Ehrlich's *The Population Bomb* and C. P. Snow's *A State of Siege* were quite alarmist and predicted catastrophic famines ahead. They were mostly mistaken. Like Thomas Malthus in his 1798 essay on population, they did not foresee technological and economic gains that would lift many people out of hunger and poverty. But they *did* get my attention.

Another thing that got my attention was the danger of ideology. A very bright friend of mine, Terry Martin, who later became one of Bread for the World's policy analysts, invited me to an evening with a couple of guests from Nicaragua, one of whom was the priest and poet Ernesto Cardenal. I had read a book of his poems based on the psalms and found them engaging. Cardenal was short, thin, and gentle, with a saintly quality. He was deeply involved with the revolutionary Sandinistas and embraced liberation theology. He spoke so effusively about Marxism and the Sandinista revolution-in-progress as an expression of his faith that I asked, "What difference do you see between Marxism and Christianity?" He replied, "Oh, there is no difference. Christians just add belief in a life hereafter." I was astonished. Terry said afterward, "Pretty naïve, isn't he?" Some forms of liberation theology are rooted in the apostolic Gospel, but Cardenal's confusion of Christianity with Marxism struck me as a huge illusion. Others confuse Christianity with capitalism, of course, but to subordinate Christian faith to *any* ideology or political view is a fatal mistake. Later, when the Sandinistas came to power, Cardenal became the minister of culture and gained some fame by his defiance of Pope John Paul II, who scolded him and later had him defrocked.

During this time the parish situation had changed. John Puelle got a call to serve a church in Mexico. He turned it down because the congregation was comprised mainly of well-to-do U.S. expatriates. But he did say he had gotten used to taking charge of the parish while I was gone and found it difficult to accept an associate's role again. If he were invited to serve a congregation more like ours, he would probably accept. I told him that if one of us left, it should be me, because the church would lose his bilingual leadership and that would probably mean the loss of our Spanish-speaking congregation. I told him that my involvement in the hunger issue seemed increasingly compelling. So I offered the possibility of my taking another leave of absence from the parish, this time to investigate the issue of hunger more seriously, and let him again assume the role of pastor. And that is what we did. Modest savings from book royalties and a $54 a month rent made this financially feasible.

I began spending most of my time reading more widely. But John Puelle and I had also made contact with the New York wing of Operation Breadbasket, led by William Jones, pastor of Bethany Baptist Church in Brooklyn. We didn't go to meetings, but we did get involved in a demonstration at the A&P supermarket headquarters in New York to urge nondiscriminatory hiring. Our group of about twenty black clergy got no response, so we staged a sit-in in the president's office that lasted into the evening and ended with arrests. My main memory of the sit-in is that of a young fourteen-year-old boy preacher by the name of Al Sharpton sitting at the president's desk, dialing the A&P president's home, and talking to his daughter. I wondered if so much attention and chutzpah at the age of fourteen could lead to any good. But the sit-in brought about changes at A&P and elsewhere.

Another group that I affiliated with while reading about hunger was the New York Clergy Coalition. This group of about two dozen Catholic, Protestant, and Jewish clergy hoped to provide an alternative to the somewhat passive Protestant Council of Churches, whose main activity, it seemed to us, was to hold an annual fund-raising dinner that attracted large donors and garnered a million dollars or so by giving a patriotism award to famous personalities, such as Bob Hope. We hoped the coalition could tackle a few real public problems. The driving force behind the coalition was Richard Neuhaus, a gifted strategist, who earlier, together with Rabbi Abraham Heschel, Father Dan Berrigan, SJ, and a few others had started Clergy Concerned about Vietnam (later Clergy and Laity Concerned), which made a highly positive contribution to the antiwar movement.

My particular assignment with the coalition was to head a small committee on prison reform. We hoped to get permission for clergy and other religious personnel to visit prisoners in New York City for cell-by-cell conversation, not just one-prisoner-only visits through a thick barrier. The commissioner of corrections denied our request. We continued to press for access, and during this time I got a call from an assistant to Louis Farrakhan of the Nation of Islam, saying, "The Honorable Minister Farrakhan would like you to visit him at his office" at the mosque on 116th Street in Harlem. I did. He was a young man in his late thirties, already seen by many as a successor to Malcolm X, who had served the same mosque prior to his assassination. The meeting was polite and proper. Farrakhan, immaculately dressed, was courteous to a fault and friendly in a formal way. He expressed great interest in gaining access to city jails. I assured him that if we gained access, it would be done on a completely nondiscriminatory basis.

I called the American Civil Liberties Union and was told by one of its lawyers that they would be happy to take the case to court. A few days later the corrections commissioner reversed himself and granted access. For a long time I went in twice a month to the Men's House of Detention ("The Tombs") in Lower Manhattan to visit a few dozen prisoners on the cellblock to which I was assigned, as did other clergy and women belonging to religious orders.

While reading mainly about hunger and poverty abroad, I learned that the noted British economist Barbara Ward would be teaching a graduate course on Third World development at Columbia University. I went to her first class and she graciously gave me permission to audit the course, to my great benefit.

I had a firsthand sense of U.S. hunger and poverty, but only from an urban perspective. I wanted to see what it was like in the rural South and Appalachia, especially in the wake of both a hair-raising 1967 report, *Hunger, USA*, by the Citizens' Board of Inquiry into Hunger and Malnutrition in the United States, and subsequent visits to the South by Senator Robert Kennedy and others. So, in the spring of 1970, Kaiya and I borrowed her mother's old Buick, and we began a five-week journey through southern states, mostly driving down back roads, knocking on rickety doors, and asking people what they faced. I was surprised at how willing and eager they were to tell their stories. Hardship, discrimination, poor health, and empty shelves abounded.

In Florida I visited a black family of nine that was eking out a living on twenty acres of land. With both parents in poor health, the family depended on government food commodities for survival. Five children went without food at school, even though lunches were offered them at the half price of fifteen cents each. The last ten days of the month this family's diet consisted of bread, syrup, and beans— beans that were cooking as we spoke, over an open hearth in ninety-degree weather because the stove in their two-and-a-half room shack no longer worked.

A white family of six in Georgia lived in a tumbledown house on a small patch of land. The house rented for $6 a month. The father could get only occasional odd jobs. The mother needed an operation, two of the youngsters were being treated for worms, and a ten-year-old girl had ulcers. Worm infestation was a common problem for youngsters in homes that lacked indoor plumbing and often contributed to malnutrition. A mother in South Carolina told me of a neighbor boy who had worms crawling out of his mouth after he died, although his death was officially attributed to pneumonia.

In Mississippi I saw a two-year-old girl with rickets, and although it was near midday, she still had not eaten. I asked her parents if they gave her milk to drink, and they said they did. I asked how often she got milk and they answered, "A couple of times a month."

I visited unpainted shanties of black farmhands working for a farmer in Arkansas who drew almost $50,000 in federal subsidies in 1969 (worth many times that in today's dollars). These laborers drove heavy equipment and did the other farm work for hourly wages that barely enabled them to squeeze out an existence for their families— that is, during the part of the year when work was needed. During the winter months they borrowed money from the owner and depended on food stamps for purchases. The arrangement made it seem as though the workers were on the government dole, and technically they were. In reality their wealthy employer was being subsidized once again, this time for not paying adequate wages, but the workers were made to bear the onus.

Putting together what I saw in the South and on the Lower East Side, I came to this conclusion: People construct their own picture of reality based on what they experience and want to believe. Widespread hunger and poverty are not part of that reality. Even when confronted with hungry people and conditions of poverty, Americans on the whole simply cannot believe or imagine the suffering because they seldom see it; when they do, it is a threat to their comfort, so they choose not to think about it. Blocking poor people from our minds, however, may be a passive way of wishing they did not exist, and it is a cause of many deaths. Perhaps that explains why a black woman in Mississippi asked me, "Do you think they are going to kill all of us?"

Shortly after our return from the South the first of our adopted sons, Nathan, arrived four months after his birth, and almost two years later, Peter at five months. It was a joyous time of life for us and we were a proud interracial family.

8

Launching Bread for the World

My work as a parish pastor on the Lower East Side required me to frequently respond to emergencies either caused or aggravated by poverty. But the harder I worked at it, the further behind I got. My father used to say, "It's better to build a fence at the top of a cliff than to have an ambulance at the bottom," and I found myself driving an ambulance most of the time. Two questions kept haunting me: What could be done to prevent people from getting caught in poverty? And, how could we enable people to work their way out? Hunger struck me as the best focus, for three reasons: First, it is an especially acute form of poverty. Second, it grabs people emotionally. Third, with exceptional power and clarity, the Bible and especially Jesus call us to help hungry people.

My study of hunger led to the writing of a couple of books. The first was a small paperback, *Breaking Bread with the Hungry.** Each topical chapter began by showing how some aspect of the problem, such as the population explosion or the environmental crisis, would eventually affect children from the ordinary midwestern town of Spencer, Iowa. I coauthored the second and more comprehensive book with my brother Paul. Its title, *The Politics of World Hunger*,† came after the book was written. We set out to describe the problem and propose solutions. We knew that the roles of private enterprise, voluntary assistance, and government are all essential. But in the case of hunger, the role of government struck us as the most neglected of the three areas. Aspects of U.S. economic and foreign policies have

---

* Arthur Simon, *Breaking Bread with the Hungry* (Minneapolis, MN: Augsburg Publishing House, 1971).

†Paul Simon and Arthur Simon, *The Politics of World Hunger* (New York, NY: Harper's Magazine Press, 1973).

a huge impact on hungry people, and those policies are determined by the government.

After submitting the manuscript of the second book to the publisher, I began to think more seriously about what could be done to get the kind of responses we thought were needed. In particular I wondered, "What could the churches do that they are not doing?" Like many other congregations, ours gave direct assistance locally and participated in supporting relief and development abroad. But it struck me that Christians were not being challenged to weigh in as citizens to help shape decisions by the government that have a huge bearing on hungry people. The nation was paying scant attention to hunger, and many of its policies were woefully inadequate. By doing little or nothing about this, Christians were silently approving those policies and reinforcing hunger.

Why not organize a citizens' outcry against hunger?

Two models occurred to me as possibly useful. First, the civil rights movement had shown me how an extreme injustice could arouse people of faith and prompt action. Second, Common Cause had recently emerged on the scene as a citizens' lobby on government reform.

These thoughts gave shape to the idea of starting a Christian citizens' movement on hunger to build public support for policies more responsive to the needs of hungry people. It could appeal to people on the basis of their faith in Christ and biblical entreaties to help those who hunger. That was the gist of my thinking. I sketched the case for it on two pages and began showing mimeographed copies to people who were either professionally engaged in antipoverty efforts or had connections that I thought might help us gain access to the churches. But I wanted to know, first of all, if people of that caliber thought the idea worth pursuing.

Responses were mixed. Some encouraged me, others did the opposite. More worrisome, among the skeptical were a few employed by the church to build support for development in poor countries. One thought I was job hunting. Some were caught up in internal disputes over the definition of development and seemed detached from any practical action. I remember meeting in a room at Riverside Church near the Protestant church center with a sizable number of curious listeners, and after I made my presentation, one of the more prominent bureaucrats said, "It sounds like an ecclesiastical Common

Cause to me." He didn't mean it as a compliment. "That's it!" I replied. "That's exactly what I have in mind—a citizens' lobby on hunger based on Christian motivation."

I had hoped for a more clear-cut, yes-or-no reaction, but what I got was uncertainty. So I decided to put the idea before Richard Neuhaus, who by this time was editing the journal *Worldview* and gaining a reputation as an observer of faith and public affairs. He had an uncanny sense of strategy, so I figured that if he didn't like the proposal, I would abandon it. If he liked it, I would go ahead. It was a bit like Gideon seeking a sign from God by laying wool on the ground to see if it would be covered with dew. Neuhaus and I had a long conversation over lunch. I gave him the paper and told him of the mixed reactions. He read it carefully. "I think you are on to something big," he said and offered to help.

With that encouragement, I began to form an organizing committee. We needed people with clear faith-and-justice commitments, a mix of knowledgeable professionals, including names that would be recognized and respected as Christian leaders. I pulled together a group of seven Roman Catholics and seven Protestants. The group included Neuhaus; Father John Calhoun, a gifted colleague from St. Brigid's, a block away from my church; Hulbert James, director of the National Council of Churches' Crusade Against Hunger; and Father William J. Byron, SJ, a member of the New York Clergy Coalition. I had a lot of respect for Byron, but knew him only as rector of the Jesuit Woodstock community in New York. I asked him if he could suggest any Catholics who might be interested in helping develop a citizens' lobby on hunger. "Yes," he said. "I would be." He had gotten his PhD in economics and was keenly aware of the hunger crisis.

For six months the committee functioned as a think tank to develop more fully the kind of organization we wanted to be. That included choosing a name. *Bread for the World* emerged as a clear favorite among several possibilities when we did some informal polling of my Christmas-card list and church members from different denominations and types of neighborhoods. Bread for the World came across as positive and nonthreatening to people, an important consideration for a group that inescapably would wade into some controversial water.

The committee agreed that our approach should be politically nonpartisan and nonideological, centered on attracting people who wanted to find practical solutions to hunger. We assumed that neither political party has a lock on the truth.

We also discussed at length the pros and cons of anchoring Bread for the World explicitly in Christian faith. Why not Christians and Jews? Or interfaith? Or why any faith at all? We based our decision to be Christian on the fact that U.S. Christians represented a vast population that was largely clueless about the use of citizenship to reduce hunger; we also believed that we could most effectively appeal to them on the basis of the faith that they treasured above all else. If we could arouse Christians to see the connection between their faith, their citizenship, and hunger, they might be willing to play an instrumental role in ending it.

The committee decided to test the idea in New York City before going national. That was an easy decision, because we had no money to begin organizing nationally. For that matter, we had only pocket change to begin locally, but one member of the committee, Gloria Fitzgerald, an Ursuline nun, volunteered to help. The two of us sent a signed letter to several thousand people in the city in which we said, "Bread for the World has no interest in promoting a politics of right, left, or center. Its concern is simply a Christian one for people who are shorn of basic human needs, and therefore it is big enough to include a wide range of viewpoints." In this and various other ways the word spread, people helped, and before long we had several-hundred members.

We tried different types of public meetings set in the context of prayer and worship. Most of these fizzled, sometimes with only one or two showing up, but we never advertised the fizzle. One thing that worked was Saturday morning sessions at the UN Church Center across the street from the United Nations. We lined up knowledgeable presenters for a variety of topics and these were well received. But we never got more than a dozen people out at any one time. Those who came, however, were not disappointed, and some have been active in Bread for decades. (Once, a group of students from Edgecliff College in Cincinnati, dropped in, led by a young professor, Connie Carroll Widmer. Connie became a charter member and later a district coordinator, and eventually she and her husband put

Bread for the World in their trust.) We built on small successes and learned from failures. The failures were discouraging, but we persisted, and I learned that persistence makes up for a multitude of limitations.

We also put out a monthly newsletter, using what to this old printer's apprentice was the stunning new technology of a Selectric IBM typewriter and offset printing. Our first newsletter, May 1973, included this paragraph:

> Why should an organization on world hunger deal with political and economic issues? Precisely because we want to show the link between hunger and poverty, between hunger and injustice. People are usually hungry because they are terribly poor. Enabling hungry people to feed themselves means dealing with the root causes of hunger. That requires us to help shape government policies, for U.S. policies often vitally affect the world's hungry. BFW wants to organize citizen participation from within the churches on their behalf.

As membership grew locally, we began to build a board of directors during our earliest years that included Norman Borlaug, Nobel Prize economist; J. Sterling Carey, president of the National Council of Churches; James Cogswell, head of the hunger program for the Presbyterian Church, U.S.A.; Owen Cooper, industrialist and past president of the Southern Baptist Convention; Sister Carol Coston, OP, director of Network; Frank Gaebelein and Paul Rees, revered evangelicals; Bishop Thomas J. Gumbleton of Detroit; Senator Mark Hatfield (R-OR); Sister Mary Luke Tobin, SL, of Church Women United; as well as Byron and Neuhaus. Pretty heavy on the male side, I'm afraid. These members and others like them gave us invaluable guidance, as well as immediate credibility.

The person we sought most of all for the board was Eugene Carson Blake, who had recently retired as general secretary of the World Council of Churches. Blake was a towering figure within mainline Protestant churches, and had been featured on the cover of *Time* magazine. Persuading him to join our board, however, was no easy task. He replied to my initial letter of invitation with a series of questions, which I answered in three full pages. To my dismay he declined, saying he was not convinced that we were truly ecumenical. I wrote a third letter, again at some length. This time he called to say he would be willing to meet me for lunch at the Princeton Club in midtown Manhattan to discuss the matter further. We explored the idea in more detail, and Blake agreed not only to serve but to become the board's first chair.

Blake gave Bread visibility and respect, but he did much more than lend his name. He made contacts with key people by letter and in person on Bread's behalf, including visits to Cardinal Cooke of New York and Bishop Mugavero of Brooklyn. He spent time with me about board and leadership matters. He preached. On a few occasions we traveled together for speaking engagements, and he and his wife Jean visited my family while we were vacationing in Vermont. He told me he would help in every way possible, "but don't expect me to ask for money." Though Blake never said so, I'm sure he recognized that I had a lot to learn, so I cherished his guidance and that of the board as a whole, and they were exceptionally generous and kind in giving it. In retrospect I am amazed at the patience that these gifted people showed, as we figured out, step by step, what to do. Our initial board set the tone for all subsequent boards in providing leadership. At no time during those thirty-five years has there been a divisive spirit on the board. Disagreements, yes, but always a sense of unity in furthering Bread's mission.

Blake made it clear that he would not have considered serving Bread had it not been explicitly Christian. He wanted to work with and through the churches, he said. However, because the World Council of Churches was "suspect" to many conservative evangelicals, he told me I would have to take the lead in cultivating them, for which my Missouri Synod affiliation was an asset.

Blake had a keen sense of the distinctive roles of the staff and the board, but he also encouraged me to use my judgment in deciding matters that might not allow time for consultation with the board. "The board will let you know if they think you've made a mistake," he said. Blake's wise and energetic leadership of the board for four years contributed greatly to Bread's strong start. When someone later complained that "things were not the way they used to be," he replied, "No, and they never were!" R. Douglas Brackenridge's biography of him, *Eugene Carson Blake: Prophet With Portfolio*, includes this paragraph:

> A major interest in his retirement years, however, has been his association with a Christian citizens' group called Bread for the World, an agency that attempts to keep elected officials informed about issues that vitally affect hungry people throughout the world. As president [board chair] of Bread for the World, Blake thought that he had at last accepted a noncontroversial position. "I soon found out," he said, "that everything worthwhile is controversial."...Blake remains adamant, however, that Bread for the World is moving in the right direction and continues to merit his full support.*

But I am getting way ahead of the story. The board had its first meeting on January 18, 1974, when going national was only a hope. We projected an initial full-year budget of $50,000 (worth about $200,000 in 2008 dollars) for hiring a staff of three, not counting money needed for bulk mailings to solicit members. At the time we had almost nothing in the bank and only a volunteer staff. We obviously had recruited a board of risk-takers.

One of the first things that Blake and Bishop Gumbleton (vice chair of the board) and I did was to meet with Jim McCracken, executive of Church World Service (a National Council of Churches entity); with Bernie Confer, executive of Lutheran World Relief; and with Jim Norris, assistant to the executive of Catholic Relief Services. Confer and Norris had already given me strong encouragement, but McCracken had suspicions. We wanted to relieve them of any doubts about the purpose of Bread for the World, and assure them that we had no intentions of competing with them by engaging in direct assistance. We promised to endorse their work, while building support for national policies that would further the goals for which their organizations existed. Gumbleton shattered my stereotype of a bishop with his gentle demeanor. And our meeting achieved its purpose.

---

* R. Douglas Brackenridge, *Eugene Carson Blake: Prophet With Portfolio*, Presbyterian Historical Society Publications 18 (New York: Seabury Press, 1978).

The previous Thanksgiving (1973), we had promoted our first campaign of letters to U.S. senators and representatives among our several-hundred members and their local churches, although with so small a membership, we could generate few messages. The letters pushed U.S. funding for the International Development Association (IDA), the "soft loan" window of the World Bank that lends money at almost no interest to the poorest countries. Perhaps your eyelids droop at my mention of this faceless economic giant, but it is the biggest single source of development aid for the least developed countries and, despite its flaws, impacts millions of impoverished people. Yet the U.S. House of Representatives not only rejected a $1.5 billion funding bill for IDA (to be spread over four years), but did so by a 248 to 155 vote, with a majority from each party turning it down. Hope of keeping funding alive depended on the Senate, so we arranged to give Bread's first congressional testimony before the Senate Foreign Relations Committee on March 22, 1974.

Blake traveled from his home in Connecticut to testify in person before the committee, and I accompanied him. He was a forceful presence. To my surprise Senator Charles Percy, the committee's ranking Republican member, introduced him warmly by saying that Blake had married Percy and his wife years earlier, when Blake was a young pastor of a Presbyterian Church in Pasadena, California. At this committee hearing, I was struck by the fact that Bread for the World appeared to be one of only two or three outside organizations presenting testimony on behalf of IDA.

Later we learned that Bread's testimony produced more of a stir than we anticipated. While strongly supportive of funding for IDA, the statement lodged a qualification regarding the channeling of IDA funds to South Vietnam. An advance copy of the testimony was sent to World Bank president, Robert S. McNamara, together with a covering letter that asked him to "clear the air" regarding rumors that the White House wanted IDA funds used heavily in South Vietnam, an indirect way of securing support for the war. A flurry of cablegrams followed, after which the Bank notified us informally that it would use a reply to us as a vehicle for distinguishing its position from that of the administration. This came in the form of a letter to Blake from Bank vice president Peter Cargill, clearly separating IDA funding from the war. I think this assurance played a possibly decisive role in the Senate's approval of funding for IDA and the House's lopsided reversal of its previous opposition, this time by a 185 to 238 vote in favor of funding.

Not many days later Blake sat in our parish house and we faced a dilemma. What were we to do? We were far short of the $50,000 we thought we needed to launch nationally. On the other hand, the media was filled with reports of regional famines. Food shortages had caused the price of grain to soar, and worries mounted that these things foreshadowed long-range catastrophes. Our plans told us to wait. My instinct told us to act. But I was afraid that Blake, the more experienced and wiser head, would advise caution. Instead he said, "If we can't get a response now, we'll never get a response."

We got the approval of the board's executive committee to plow all of our money into a mailing of 68,000 letters announcing Bread for the World's birth and urging people to join. We used subscription lists of four periodicals, each of which had tested well in our local solicitation of members—*Commonweal* and *The National Catholic Reporter* on the Catholic side and *The Christian Century* and *Christianity & Crisis* on the Protestant side. All four publications had two things in common: roots in Christian faith and a strong orientation toward social justice.

We hoped and we prayed.

And we waited anxiously.

The letters went out in mid-May. Our board met for the second time on the afternoon of May 20. That morning the mail brought in the first batch of returns: eighty-seven new members at $10 each. That was the moment I sensed our leap of faith was working, because I knew those returns were just the tip of an iceberg. Within a few weeks we had two-thousand members and Bread was growing rapidly.

9

Watching It Rise

You may think that leading Bread for the World was what I had in mind from the very beginning, but in that case you would be quite mistaken. I neither wanted nor expected to serve as its executive, for good reasons. I had never taken a course in economics or political science. My administrative experience and skills were limited. I had never set foot in a poor country. I do not have the personality of a strong leader, and no one ever accused me of being a charismatic speaker—in fact a Denver parishioner once told me, "Pastor, your sermons aren't long, they just *seem* long." I wanted to help launch Bread for the World not because I was especially well prepared to do so, but because the need was so great.

I planned to return to parish ministry. During the time that we were still giving the idea of Bread for the World a trial run in New York City, I served for a while as an interim pastor on Sundays at St. Paul's Lutheran Church in Tremont, a low-income section of the Bronx, and found doing so thoroughly enjoyable. A few of the folks there asked me if I would be willing to have my name put forward as a candidate they might consider "calling" as their permanent pastor. I wanted to say yes, but felt a responsibility to see Bread for the World through, if possible, to its launching nationally, so I declined.

At its initial meeting in January 1974 the board of directors agreed to let me advertise for a chief executive. Despite our uncertain future, several dozen applied—all men, as I recall—and a committee offered the best of these to the board at its meeting in May. Blake asked me to leave the room and to my surprise the board elected me executive director (a title later changed to president). We were carving out new territory and board members promised to work with me in figuring out how to do it.

Up to this point we relied on volunteers. These included Jeanne Wilhelm, a Franciscan nun who typed membership records on 3-by-5 cards, and Dan Sendzig, who managed various office duties. Both later became part of our staff.

I hired Joel Underwood to help organize and equip our growing membership. Joel had served as a Methodist missionary in India, but was currently working with the International Documentation on the Contemporary Churches, which published documents coming mainly from churches in developing countries. He served Bread effectively for twenty-five years and directed three different departments before he retired.

Brennon Jones became our first policy analyst. He had worked for Church World Service in Vietnam as a conscientious objector, found his niche there as a journalist, did research on Indochina for CBS News, then became research-and-production manager for the Academy Award–winning documentary on Vietnam *Hearts and Minds*, for which his fluency in Vietnamese was critical. Brennon took the lead on several of our major campaigns during our earliest years, and has since had a distinguished global career as a journalist and editor, and also in peace-keeping and humanitarian work for the United Nations. As I write, he is living in Bangkok establishing South and Southeast Asia operations for IRIN, the UN humanitarian news service.

We also needed a policy analyst based in Washington, DC, and I hired another journalist who had experience abroad with churches in poor countries. Barbara Howell was so gentle that I wondered if she could withstand the rigors of Capitol Hill. She soon allayed my fears and became one of the nation's best informed and most effective advocates on domestic hunger. She served us more than twenty-five years. I learned quickly that the best policy analysts are those with the instincts of an investigative reporter.

The hiring of these early staff members was clearly providential. I had never before hired anyone and the decision in each case could easily have backfired, so I am profoundly grateful to God for undeserved guidance as well as to these staff members for their stellar service, without which Bread would have stumbled. Later, I learned through mistakes to screen candidates carefully, and I take that learning to be providential as well.

I also learned not to hire *over*qualified staff. One exciting addition was Francis X. Murphy, a seasoned Redemptorist priest, famous in many circles as Xavier Rynne, who under that pseudonym had written a series of thirteen informative articles for *The New Yorker* magazine during the 1960s on developments behind the scenes at the Vatican II Council. He was a delightful presence, but soon found irresistible an offer to join Sargent Shriver on an extended trip to investigate religious and political matters in the Soviet Union. Then a year or so later, when we were looking for our first director of communications, a young man named Tom Cahill came to my office applying for the post. It was apparent that he had exceptional literary gifts, while we needed someone mainly to write copy for the newsletter and edit background papers. I told him that I would hire him on the spot, if he insisted, but that in a few weeks he would probably go crazy and find a better way to use his talent. He agreed, and before long he and his wife Susan started a high-quality publishing venture, and he is currently writing his fifth book about "the seven hinges of history," each of which so far has been a best seller. The first one, *How the Irish Saved Civilization*, sold more than a million copies the first year. Over the years Cahill has spoken out for Bread on many occasions.

From the very start I proposed that we pay salaries on the basis of need rather than position. We did so for two reasons. First, we had little money. Second, it seemed to me that pay based on need was consistent with our work as an antihunger organization. My own family was living in a $54-a-month apartment, so our needs were limited, and I saw no reason why I should be getting a hefty paycheck. My salary at Bread never reached the level earned by that of an average elementary school teacher and sometimes fell below that of our mailroom clerk. This policy served us well for more than a decade, gave us a talented staff, and allowed Bread to do more with its income than would otherwise have been possible. Eventually the policy had to be adjusted, as I will explain later.

From the outset we developed a consensus style of working together on the staff. This tapped the strengths that others on staff had to contribute, but it also reflected my own limitations. We were all figuring out how best to further a new movement that was suddenly mushrooming. For the most part, this method worked well. It certainly gave the staff a sense of ownership and nourished a high level of commitment, though it did not always bring about clean lines of administration—a weakness of mine. Founders are typically better at launching an idea than in administering it. I could give you a few examples, but this is not a warts-and-all book, so you will have to accept that I had a lot to learn about administration. At one early point a board member arranged an invitation for me to attend a six-week, invitation-only session at Harvard for promising but inexperienced administrators, and I declined, thinking too many opportunities would be neglected. In retrospect I missed a chance that a wiser person would have seized.

The hiring of staff required a move to larger quarters than the rooms we shared with the church in our tiny parish building. George (Bill) Webber, president of New York Theological Seminary on East 49th Street in Manhattan, offered us space at very low rent in the seminary building. Webber once told me, long before Bread began, "You have to decide whether you want to take credit or get something done. If you don't worry about taking credit, you can get a lot done." It was advice I remembered often, although carried out inconsistently, but I don't recall ever having regretted using it. One example of Webber's leadership grew out of the Attica, New York, prison uprising in 1971. The seminary started a theological training program for prisoners at the Sing Sing prison for long-term felons, and by 2008 more than four hundred prisoners had graduated from its master's degree program, many of them now ordained ministers. I wonder why more seminaries don't do this.

While at our East 49th Street headquarters, I got a call from Eileen Egan, one of our board members. Eileen was a remarkable, saintly woman who worked most of her adult life and long into retirement for Catholic Relief Services, primarily for refugees. She was closely tied to the Catholic Worker movement and a dear friend of Dorothy Day. Eileen cofounded Pax Christi USA, a peace organization, and was the one who coined the term *seamless garment* to describe Catholic issues regarding respect for human life. A biographer of Mother Teresa, Eileen served as her guide on trips to the United States. Eileen called to tell me that Mother Teresa was in her office and wanted to meet me. Could I come? That gave me a half hour of conversation with just the three of us. Mother Teresa was interested in Bread, knew Senator Hatfield as one of our board members, and told me of his visit to Calcutta and his hands-on work at her

House of the Dying. At one point in the conversation, I mentioned that poverty in India was more extreme than in the United States. She startled me by saying, "Yes, but in your country you have a much bigger problem. Your children are often starving for lack of love."

During this time Bread for the World was growing at a healthy clip. We had 5,736 paid members by the end of 1974, and 9,400 in May 1975, a year after our national launching. We had coverage everywhere within the church it seemed—publications, newsletters, networks, and word of mouth. The idea was taking hold. Although we were underrepresented in the South, and among minority groups and conservative evangelicals, we were gaining members in those areas as well.

Paulist Press played a huge role in helping Bread grow. Not long after I was hired, the board suggested that I write an easily understood introduction to hunger and our mission. The result was a paperback entitled *Bread for the World*,* which I was able to write in a few months because I had gathered most of the raw material earlier while writing *The Politics of World Hunger* with my brother Paul. Paulist Press agreed to be the lead publisher, with Eerdmans as copublisher, and seven weeks after receiving my manuscript, Paulist produced a 180-page paperback that sold for $1.50 each.

Paulist staff also came up with a breathtaking promotion plan. They sent a free copy to each of 17,000 Catholic parishes in the United States. They offered to send as many free copies as any parish wanted for distribution to their parishioners as they left Sunday Mass, with an insert in each book asking people either to return the book the following Sunday or pay for it. This resulted in the sale of tens of thousands of books, plus thousands of new Bread members, along with a lot of talk, excitement, and reviews in various publications. The book also benefited from strong endorsements by prominent figures, including Gunnar Myrdal, the Nobel Prize–winning Swedish economist, famous for *An American Dilemma*, his monumental two-volume analysis of racism in our nation, which helped lay groundwork for the civil rights movement. I had sent Myrdal the manuscript of my book thinking it unlikely that he would read it. But he did, and endorsed it as a "clear and convincing" analysis of hunger.

---

* Arthur Simon, *Bread for the World* (New York/Mahwah, NJ: Paulist Press, 1975).

The book won a National Religious Book Award the following year, and it continued to attract new members for a long time. Rick Steves, author of the *Europe through the Back Door* books and host of the PBS travel program *Rick Steves' Europe*, told me that when he was a young man, he was walking down a Seattle street when a stranger came up to him and handed him a copy of *Bread for the World*. He read it, got hooked, and said, "It made me aware of the economic and political connections to hunger, and I became an activist Christian."

With hunger in the news, and Bread for the World getting considerable attention, I was invited for occasional TV interviews, once on an hour-long NBC network program with Father Theodore Hesburgh, CSC, president of Notre Dame, and Rabbi Marc Tanenbaum of the American Jewish Committee. More surprising to me was an invitation to appear on Pat Robertson's talk show, the *700 Club*. I think it surprised Pat Robertson even more, because when I explained Bread's work as a citizens' lobby, he began belittling the role of government. His father, he said, had served in the U.S. Senate from Virginia, and he, Pat, had worked on a Senate committee as a young man, and he deplored its ineptness. I argued that the government had a great impact on hungry people and needed to be improved and strengthened for that purpose, not downgraded. I could sense his discomfort as he cut the interview short and moved on to the next segment of the program. Someone on his staff, I'm confident, got chewed out for not doing his homework.

From the very start the board played an exceptionally creative role in giving shape to Bread. As Bread began taking off, we asked, "What are we going to do with all these new members? How are we going to find volunteer leaders for states and congressional districts?" The board's own answer was Project 500—an effort to recruit and train 500 activists to spearhead our work. We immediately began preparing a series of regional seminars, and out of them we recruited hundreds of leaders.

In Texas, for example, we got Pat Ayres. She had been involved in inner-city work with children and served on a juvenile justice commission. She had become embittered by the racial and economic injustices she saw, but gave her life to Christ when she saw two streams—the Gospel and justice—converge. After visiting a number of poor countries with her family, including the various ministries of Mother Teresa's Missionaries of Charity in Calcutta, she returned deeply moved. Phil Strickland of the Texas Baptist Christian Life Commission encouraged her to attend one of our Project 500 weekend seminars where, she said, "It all came together. I had been linking concern and action, faith and finance, and Bread for the World gave me a vision of how to do that more effectively through advocacy." Pat volunteered to be a congressional district coordinator, then state coordinator, and eventually served for several years as chair of our board. She and her husband Bob, former president of the University of the South, have been actively involved in Bread ever since that eye-opening seminar.

Tony Cernera and Tom Forget, recent college graduates, attended our New York Project 500 retreat. They grabbed the reigns of leadership in building an active Bread for the World chapter in New York City. About a year later we persuaded them to join the staff, Tony as an assistant to the director of Bread for the World Institute (then called the Educational Fund), and Tom as a regional organizer. Both excelled. Tony eventually became director of the Institute. Both left the staff for family reasons when we relocated to the nation's capital some years later. Tony is now president of Sacred Heart University in Fairfield, Connecticut (where Tom serves as academic dean), as well as president of the International Federation of Catholic Universities—the only American besides Father Ted Hesburgh of Notre Dame to ever hold that position. The leadership of these people in Bread, along with that of several-hundred others who became the backbone of our growing network, came about as a result of Project 500 seminars.

John Connor, pastor of a town-and-university Presbyterian church in Corvallis, Oregon, attended one of our seminars in Portland. John was a short, round man with a contagious smile, blessed with a great heart for hungry people. He began buying our book in such quantities that at the seminar he told me he had given away 1,700 copies to Presbyterians throughout the Northwest. That gave us a jump start in the region. John had a wonderful sense of humor, and as a few of us were talking late one evening and laughing at some of his stories, he told us he planned to run for moderator of his denomination. I roared with laughter, thinking it another joke. But John insisted that he was serious. Sure enough, before a year went by he had been elected moderator. He continued to be a missionary for Bread and hungry people until death cut his life short at an early age a few years later.

In these and other ways Bread grew in numbers and in better-equipped members.

10

The Right to Food

On May 20, 1974, when Bread for the World's membership began to lift off, the nation was still at war in Vietnam, and the mushrooming Watergate scandal prompted *Time* magazine to feature "Nixon's Shattered Presidency" on its cover. But under the news radar, other events were shaping Bread's path.

The Overseas Development Council convened a group of a hundred church leaders and antipoverty specialists at the Aspen (Colorado) Institute. Eugene Carson Blake and I were among those invited by James P. Grant, founder and president of the council, to participate in this consultation, which gave Bread additional visibility and valuable contacts. Grant, a visionary leader, would soon play an extraordinary role on the world scene as director of the United Nation's Children's Fund (UNICEF). He was one of the persons to whom I had sent a copy of my proposal about forming a Christian citizens' movement on hunger. While many didn't bother to respond, Grant was so taken by the idea that one evening while in New York, he took a taxi to the Lower East Side (against the advice of the cab driver) and bounded up four flights of stairs to my fifth-floor tenement apartment to offer his encouragement. That was typical of Jim Grant.

Robert McNamara, World Bank president, also participated in the Aspen consultation. Perhaps haunted by his role as secretary of defense during the early Vietnam War–years, he became emotional when he spoke about the suffering of those living in absolute poverty and could not hold back tears. To my surprise, he sought me out at the consultation to thank me for Bread's support of the International Development Association, the World Bank's main antipoverty arm, before the Senate Foreign Relations Committee (see chapter 8). We had only a few-hundred members at the time of the Senate hearing, so McNamara's response strengthened my feeling that Bread could make an impact way out of proportion to its numbers.

Famines and threat of famine were big news in 1974 and, as the Overseas Development Council consultation illustrated, they spawned events and initiatives for which the launching of Bread in May of that year was well timed. By far the most important of these was the November 1974 UN World Food Conference, which brought together high-level delegations from 132 nations to Rome. It urged landmark initiatives, among them an international system of food reserves, an early warning system for famine prevention, and establishment of the International Fund for Agricultural Development designed to boost food production and living standards of impoverished farm families. At this conference, U.S. Secretary of State Henry Kissinger proposed, and the nations resolved, "that within a decade no child will go to bed hungry." He went on to say that, for the first time in history, humankind had the technology and the resources to overcome hunger, and if we failed to do so, failure would result not from lack of ability, but lack of will.

The next month President Ford commissioned the National Academy of Sciences to determine what scientific contributions the United States ought to make. The academy published the six-volume *World Food and Nutrition Study* in 1977 that included many recommendations; it also noted that lack of political will, not technology, was the main obstacle. "If there is the political will in this country and abroad,...it should be possible to overcome the worst aspects of widespread hunger and malnutrition within one generation," the report concluded.*

Both the UN World Food Conference and the academy's report were trumpeting two salient points that prompted Bread's mission: (1) that the solution to world hunger is within our grasp, because progress had already shown that we have the resources and ability to end hunger; and (2) that the remaining uncertainty is the political will to do it. We wanted to mobilize citizens to build that political will. You'd think that followers of Jesus would jump at the chance.

---

* National Academy of Sciences, *World Food and Nutrition Study* (Washington, DC: National Research Council, 1977).

Around the time of the World Food Conference, a group of religious denominations with Washington offices established the Interreligious Task Force on U.S. Food Policy, under the leadership of George Chauncey. Each of the mostly mainline Protestant offices in this coalition dealt with a wide range of issues, but agreed to work together within the task force on food policy. However, the task force was not allowed to build a grassroots membership to support its positions, because that was already the work of another mostly mainline Protestant group called Impact, which had a membership base of about 5,000 and lobbied on many issues. This frustrated the task force, which felt that its hands were tied. A few years later, the two groups did merge, but the combined entity eventually folded. Bread for the World saw the task force as an important partner, both before and after the merger, but we had the great advantages of a rapidly growing membership base and a less complicated structure.

Shortly after the World Food Conference, the National Council of Churches held a retreat on the hunger crisis to which Blake and I were invited, along with a hundred or so representatives of the various council member churches and agencies. We broke into small groups. Everybody's ideas, hundreds of them, soon covered the walls. It wasn't clear to me how any of them could be implemented, but the retreat did stir awareness and helped spawn various initiatives. Bread for the World, up and running by that time, was recognized as a significant partner of the churches, and I think the retreat reinforced that perception, along with respect for the fact that our membership was made up of Roman Catholics and conservative evangelicals, as well as mainline Protestants.

The Right to Food—Bread's Policy

Although Bread for the World's approach to hunger was fairly clear, a more detailed "working statement of policy" was sent to the membership in August 1975 under the title "The Right to Food." It began:

Our response to the hunger crisis springs from God's love for all people. By creating us and redeeming us through Jesus Christ, he has given us a love that will not turn aside from those who lack daily bread. The human wholeness of all of us—the well fed as well as the starving—is at stake.

As Christians we affirm the right to food: the right of every man, woman, and child on earth to a nutritionally adequate diet. This right is grounded in the value God places on human life and in the belief that "the earth is the Lord's and the fullness thereof."

The statement included the following objectives, each with an explanation:

1. An end to hunger in the United States
2. A U.S. food policy committed to world food security and rural development
3. The reform and expansion of U.S. development assistance
4. The separation of development assistance from all forms of military assistance
5. Trade preferences for the poorest countries
6. Reduced military spending
7. Study and appropriate control of multinational corporations, with particular attention to agribusiness
8. Efforts to deal with the population growth rate
9. Christian patterns of living

While recognizing the necessity of responding to famines and other emergencies, the statement emphasized structural changes more than assistance, and long-term strategies more than emergency aid, so that people would have the opportunity to work their way out of hunger and poverty. Assistance, it said, "should be aimed at developing self-reliance, not dependency on the part of recipient nations and people."

Though the statement's nine points may seem to have the nurturing aura of motherhood, each moved us into territory that stepped on economic or political toes of one kind or another. Blake's biographer (see chapter 8) notes that when Blake took on a leadership role at Bread, he was brought into conflict with those who think that assisting hungry people will only make more of them starve later.

Blake was referring to Bread's position on population growth, which read, in part:

> Rapid population growth is putting great pressure on the world's food supply and on the capacity of countries to absorb the increase into their economies. Population growth will not be effectively curbed if it is dealt with in isolation, but only if placed in the context of total development needs. For example, hungry people usually have large families, in part because surviving sons provide security in old age. Only where social and economic gains include the poor, and where the rate of infant mortality begins to approximate that of the affluent nations, do people feel secure enough to limit family size.

We decided to tackle the criticism head-on when a group called the Environmental Fund published a full-page ad in *The New York Times* and *The Wall Street Journal* entitled "The Real Crisis Behind the 'Food Crisis.'" Its signatories included Garrett Hardin, who originated "lifeboat ethics" (that is, if we pull more people into our lifeboat, we'll all sink), and other prominent figures. It said the real problem is not hunger, but population because "food production cannot keep pace with the galloping growth of population." It said that family planning cannot and will not check this runaway growth, implying the need for unspecified government coercion.

Bread for the World reprinted the ad in a background paper entitled "Debate on Hunger." The paper gave a point-by-point rebuttal of the ad, maintaining that hunger is more cause than consequence of population growth. The president of the Environmental Fund attacked Bread's position, during testimony before a subcommittee of the House International Relations Committee. Bread for the World was invited to respond, which we did, again point-by-point. Because our "Debate on Hunger" paper was widely circulated among development groups and in church circles, it helped remove some misconceptions and strengthened Bread's reputation. I should add that, although population growth continues to be a big problem in many countries, the overall *rate* of growth has sharply fallen. In developing countries as a whole, the average number of children born to a woman during her childbearing years in 1974 was six. Today it is three. The Fund's assertion that food production could not keep pace with population growth was not only wrong at the time, but has proved false during subsequent decades. That could change, of course, as the galloping growth of affluence (along with population growth) drives up demand for food and energy.

The Right to Food—
A National Campaign

The "right to food" framed Bread's policy statement. It also became the focus of our first big national campaign, and marked the first time that, in collaboration with congressional sponsors, we helped draft a proposal that was introduced in Congress. Senator Mark Hatfield, an Oregon Republican and a member of our board, became chief sponsor on the Senate side, and Representative Donald Fraser, a Democrat from Minnesota, the chief sponsor in the House. The proposal was introduced as the *Right to Food Resolution*—not to be confused with Bread's statement of policy with an almost identical name.

The right to food, as we saw it, is not a right that we demand from God, but a reflection of the obligation we have toward one another before God. It is implicit in the Declaration of Independence and explicit in UN declarations. We wanted it to arouse Congress and the nation.

The resolution began:

> Whereas in this Bicentennial Year we reaffirm our national commitment to the inalienable right of all to life, liberty, and the pursuit of happiness, none of which can be realized without food to adequately sustain and nourish life, and we recall that the right to food and freedom from hunger was set forth in the Universal Declaration of Human Rights and in the World Food Conference Declaration of 1974....

Among other things the resolution declared it to be the sense of Congress that "the need to combat hunger shall be a fundamental point of reference in the formulation and implementation of the United States policy in all areas which bear on hunger including international trade, monetary arrangements, and foreign assistance."*

A resolution is not law and therefore not binding, which caused some to dismiss it as "simply a resolution." But consider the Declaration of Independence. The great themes of life, liberty, and equality set forth in the Declaration have often been ignored and violated, but they set a standard for which to strive and against which performance can be measured, and it has been a powerful agent of change. The Declaration, in short, gives us a promise to live up to. That's what we wanted to accomplish with the *Right to Food Resolution*.

When the resolution was introduced in the fall of 1975, Congress paid no attention to it. Roughly five thousand bills introduced in Congress that year never passed and its members had not the faintest idea about the vast majority of them. Our resolution seemed destined to be among those ignored. Then letters we had set in motion started arriving in congressional offices—first a trickle, then a flow, and soon a small avalanche. And as the letters mounted, they stirred attention. Members of Congress were alerted to the *Right to Food Resolution*: public interest had attracted their attention.

How did Bread for the World, with a membership of about twelve thousand when the resolution was introduced, manage to drum up ten or fifteen times that many letters to Congress within a year?

The answer lies in our connection to the churches and our instrument of an annual "Offering of Letters." The Offering of Letters is a way of inviting parishioners to "contribute" by writing to their members of Congress about a specific hunger issue, and then offering the letters in church, usually during worship. In this way, we visibly offer to God the power we have to help shape government policies that can enable hungry people to feed themselves. This use of citizenship is part of the whole of life that is meant to be given to God and a way of reflecting God's love and justice. We had promoted letter campaigns before—in 1973 supporting the International Development Association (see chapter 8) when Bread was just testing the water. We did it again for Thanksgiving 1974 on a nationwide basis in support of the

---

* House Concurrent Resolution 737 and Senate Concurrent Resolution 138, 1975.

UN World Food Conference recommendations, but on a relatively modest scale.

This time, however, we pulled out all the stops. We now had the attention of major church leaders and thousands of churches; a larger, growing, and more experienced membership and staff; and more resources to work with. Hunger was still in the news, churches were getting more actively involved, and people had become increasingly concerned. The idea of a right to food had strong moral appeal. Many denominational offices were eager to get their congregations to do an Offering of Letters and began promoting it. We were also able to get an unprecedented range of religious leaders, including evangelist Billy Graham and New York's Cardinal Terence Cooke, as well as Jewish leaders, to announce their joint support of the resolution. These endorsements hit the news and triggered additional mail to Congress. On April 8 *The Wall Street Journal* applauded the religious leaders and printed a lead editorial entitled "The Right to Food." On June 25 *The Washington Post* showed pictures of Blake, Bishop James S. Rausch of the U.S. Catholic Conference, and Rabbi Marc Tanenbaum, with an article about their congressional testimony supporting the resolution and their expression of alarm at foot-dragging by the Ford administration. The resolution had attracted a growing coalition of support.

That's the way the big picture looked, but the big picture was built on the work of thousands of ordinary folks who wrote letters to their U.S. senators and representatives. Kitty Schaller of New Jersey, for example, had become a Bread activist and was serving as our volunteer coordinator in her congressional district. She wrote to her congresswoman, Millicent Fenwick, an influential Republican, who opposed the resolution. Fenwick favored private aid instead of government action, so she proposed a "duty to share" resolution that featured charity rather than justice. Kitty challenged her position in a letter to the editor of a local newspaper. Early one morning Kitty was awakened by the ringing of her phone. The conversation* went something like this:

This is Millicent Fenwick. Is this Kitty Schaller?"

"Yes," replied Kitty, waking up fast.

---

* Kitty Schaller citation used with permission.

"How dare you write that letter!" Fenwick said, in an unusual display of anger toward a constituent. She then explained her opposition to the resolution.

Kitty told Fenwick why she thought food should be recognized as a right that entailed public responsibility, not left entirely to the whims of private charity. As they exchanged viewpoints, the conversation became friendlier. Fenwick thanked Kitty, but indicated no change of mind. We had no idea at the time how important that phone call by and the continuing flow of letters to Fenwick would be.

Public and congressional support for the resolution kept mounting, but the resolution was stuck in the House and Senate agriculture committees. I talked to my brother Paul, by then a U.S. congressman from Illinois. Paul had become a good friend of Senator Hubert Humphrey (D-MN), who served on the Senate Agriculture Committee. Humphrey bent the ear of Herman Talmadge (D-GA) who chaired the committee, and by dint of friendship or political capital or both, he got Talmadge to bring it to the committee for a vote. Paul called me on September 16 to say that Humphrey had just gotten off the phone and said, "Tell your brother the resolution went through the committee and has been approved by the full Senate."

That still left us with a problem on the House side. I met with Tom Foley, chairman of the House Agriculture Committee and later Speaker of the House. Foley was personally favorable and wanted to help. But he told me, "Some members of my committee say that a *Right to Food Resolution* is okay. But if we do that, the next thing you know they are going to come along and tell us, 'That means we need to have a grain reserve.'" In fact, grain reserves were exactly what we had decided to seek in our next major campaign, but that was no time to announce it, so I said nothing.

Foley got his committee to relinquish jurisdiction over the resolution and let the International Relations Committee handle it. Meanwhile the State Department had sent a message to Congress that said, "The executive branch questions both the desirability and feasibility of worldwide right to food as a cornerstone of U.S. policy." With time running out, we feared that Fenwick's opposition could stall action in the committee or make it difficult to achieve the required two-thirds majority in the House. Then at the last minute, Fenwick unexpectedly spoke out in favor of the resolution, crediting constituents for helping her see it in a different way. It sailed through the committee, and on September 21, 1976, the House of Representatives approved it by a vote of 340 to 61.

But that is only part of the story. Fenwick became a staunch supporter of grain reserves, and a few years later she was appointed by President Reagan to be the U.S. ambassador to the U.N. food agencies in Rome, where she served as an advocate for more enlightened food policies within the administration. Kitty Schaller and the others in her district who had written letters to Fenwick impacted the lives of countless hungry people in ways they could never have imagined. Small actions led to big consequences. Kitty calls her role in the campaign "a life-changing experience," and she now directs the Manna Food Bank in Asheville, North Carolina.

The Right to Food campaign gave a big boost to the idea that citizen advocacy could shape public policy and move the nation to act against hunger. It became a rallying point for churches and church bodies who were beginning to address hunger. The campaign also proved to be a great membership recruiter for Bread and helped to put us on the map.

Our early success inspired related efforts. Sam Daley-Harris, a young music teacher in the Los Angeles area, became an active Bread member and began organizing a network of followers to push our policy agenda. They soon formed their own lobby on hunger called Results, which continued to adopt our material for a couple of years until it became financially able to develop its own. Results is still an active partner of Bread on many issues, and I am grateful for it. Sam saw the importance of helping poor people become small-scale entrepreneurs, so he started a Microcredit Summit Campaign that has successfully convened several international assemblies of practitioners who specialize in giving small loans so very poor people can start very small businesses. Sam deserves macrocredit for this, but I like to think of his work, in part at least, as one of the by-products of Bread.

Another promising idea that Bread's success may have encouraged was the launching in October 1976 of New Directions, a group promoting citizen action on U.S. foreign policy, with special concern for developing countries. Jim Grant of the Overseas Development Council, Norman Cousins of literary fame, and Father Ted Hesburgh of Notre Dame were among the towering figures behind it. Its executives (one at a time) included two former governors and a retired congressman. It was heavily funded and prominently announced by the media. I thought it might compete with us for members, but help achieve our goals. However, it had trouble catching on. Grant invited me to serve on its board, so at my first meeting I suggested changing the name. "New Directions" was a congressional mandate in 1973 for focusing U.S. foreign aid more directly on basic human needs in poor countries—the right idea, I thought, but not a name for sending a clear message to people. New directions for what? Travel? Love? Choosing a career? Anthropologist Margaret Meade immediately let me know that they had already gone down that path and had no desire to revisit it. So with an additional grant, they mailed another million glossy invitations that got few returns, and New Directions folded. The effort had been almost the mirror opposite of ours—lots of money and prelaunch publicity, but little connection with the grass roots.

11

The Fight for Food

During the summer of 1976, presidential politics dominated the news. Jimmy Carter had swept the Democratic primaries and, with the nomination all but officially in hand, was gearing up to run against President Ford. I was invited to visit the new Carter headquarters in Atlanta and meet with Stuart Eizenstat, who became Carter's chief domestic policy advisor. I encountered empty rooms with no furniture, and stacks of position papers on the floor. The only two people present were Eizenstat and a younger brother, who was apparently volunteering to help with the move. My main purpose was to urge Carter to give the problem of domestic and world hunger strong presidential leadership, should he be elected. I also wanted to explain my concern that a prominently mentioned policy advisor of Carter had signed that awful Environmental Fund ad about hunger and population that I mentioned in chapter 10.

Shortly afterward, I went on vacation to Vermont with my family, where each year we stayed in a small cabin near Lake Champlain, thanks to the generosity of Mary Doten, a marvelous, old, retired schoolteacher. The *Right to Food Resolution*, while gaining momentum in Congress as a whole, awaited action in the agriculture committees. I was happy to get away for a couple of weeks to enjoy the beach and hiking trails with Kaiya and our sons Nathan, age five, and Peter, almost four.

My vacation was interrupted by a phone call from the Carter headquarters. One of his aides told me that Carter wanted to spend a day on retreat with religious leaders to discuss the problem of hunger, and asked if Bread for the World would take the lead on this. He said Carter wanted Eugene Carson Blake to chair the session and asked if we would be willing to pull together about a dozen participants. The group had to include Jewish and Roman Catholic leaders, as well as a cross section of Protestants. The Catholic leadership would be particularly important and possibly difficult to arrange, he cautioned.

I was elated. Here was an offer for Bread to take a leading role on hunger from the man who might become the next president. We had opened doors to many religious leaders with our work on the *Right to Food Resolution*, which no doubt had much to do with Carter's invitation, so I was confident that we could handle it. After notifying Blake, I called Msgr. Thomas Kelly, newly installed as general secretary for the Catholic bishops. His predecessor, Bishop James Rausch, had helped get the endorsements of Cardinal Terence Cooke and Archbishop Joseph Bernardin for the *Right to Food Resolution*, and Kelly seemed eager to pursue Carter's invitation. He said he would first have to consult Bernardin, president of the U.S. Catholic bishops.

Kelly later called back, only to report the wrenching news that, with great regret, Bernardin felt obligated to decline the invitation. Carter's stance on abortion had become a bone of contention. Ford had endorsed a constitutional amendment to ban abortions, and Carter said he was personally opposed to abortion but felt it could be better curbed by other means. The Catholic bishops did not want to be seen as weakening their opposition to abortion by joining with Carter during the campaign, even on the issue of hunger. It was the most painful setback I ever had at Bread. But I also understood and was sympathetic to the dilemma that Bernardin faced. Perhaps the bishops had agreed that Carter was off-limits to them for a while, though I fervently wished Bernardin could have found a way in this instance of affirming life regarding hunger, while doing the same on abortion—a "seamless garment" approach. I should add that Bernardin was supportive of Bread in other ways and wrote an endorsement for a book I later did about harvesting peace at the end of the Cold War. Still, the invitation from Carter was a great opportunity lost, a huge fish that got away.

Despite this disappointment, we were encouraged to know that a Carter administration would be favorably disposed to initiatives against hunger. During Carter's first year in office, we launched a campaign of letters urging the president to lay before Congress "far-reaching proposals that would move this country and the world toward the elimination of hunger and the poverty that causes it." We reported to our members: "The grandest idea circulating in and about the Carter administration is to alleviate the abysmal poverty gripping the lives of the billion most wretched people in the world....But it is still unclear whether more than token ways to do this will be found." In November Carter appointed a White House working group to make recommendations on hunger and was said to consider presenting proposals in a special address to Congress. By mid-January 1978, one year into the Carter administration, the White House reported that it was getting more mail on hunger than on any other single issue.

Carter, however, felt badgered by opposition to a number of other proposals, including one on welfare reform, so he announced that he would make few if any new ones for a long time. To keep the issue of hunger alive in the White House, we and others urged the president to appoint a commission to make recommendations. He did so later that year. Brennon Jones, Bread policy analyst, worked closely with its staff and testified before the commission. Because the commission members represented both political parties and a variety of views, its report contained elements of compromise, but its implementation would have put the nation light years ahead in its response to hunger. Its central recommendation was "that the United States Government make the elimination of hunger the primary focus of its relationships with the developing countries." Imagine how different the world might be today had that recommendation taken hold.

Bread for the World Institute was one of several groups that received a grant from the U.S. Agency of International Development to inform the public regarding the report. The grant enabled us to hold seven regional seminars around the country, preparing people for leadership against hunger. Our links with the Carter administration seemed to put us within reach of advancing toward some of our goals. But by the time the commission's report came out in March of 1980, Carter was facing an uphill struggle for reelection, so its recommendations never got the attention and perhaps the action they might have received had he won a second term.

The Fight for a Grain Reserve

In the wake of food shortages and regional famines, the 1974 World Food Conference had urged the establishment of a global network of national grain reserves for the purpose of responding to emerging food crises. While Congress was still considering the *Right to Food Resolution*, Bread for the World had decided that its next major campaign would seek a large farmer-owned grain reserve, along with a smaller government-owned reserve for responding to emergencies abroad. The U.S. role was crucial. Because the United States was by far the world's largest grain exporter, the price and supply of grain in our country had impact on the price and availability of grain worldwide.

Grain reserves seemed a critical need, but we faced the opposition of some powerful farm organizations, partly because the government had established a reserve in the 1950s from which it began to release grain when farm prices were low, further depressing prices and driving many farmers into bankruptcy. So farmers had an understandable suspicion of what a grain reserve might do to their livelihood.

In consultation with John A. Schnittker and other leading agricultural economists, we proposed legislation for a grain reserve owned by farmers and held on their farms, with the government paying only for the storage. Farmers would fill the reserve when the price of grain was low, and sell when the price reached a predetermined high point. This would help to prevent the price of grain from getting either too high or too low, because grain released from the reserve at a high point would put more grain on the market and keep the price in check; grain purchased to replenish the reserve when the price got low would keep some grain off the market and tend to lift the price. In this way both farmers and consumers would be protected from the boom-and-bust cycle that periodically either bankrupted farmers or caused people to go hungry.

The proposal was not a cure-all, but we had reason to believe it would help farmers, as well as consumers, and offer some protection against hunger. We found House and Senate sponsors for the idea and launched another Offering of Letters campaign. Two of our three policy analysts worked on it. Brennon Jones wrote opinion pieces that appeared in major newspapers. Terry Martin was interviewed on PBS's McNeil-Lehrer news program, and at Texas A&M, I went back-to-back (or toe-to-toe) with Alan Grant, president of the National Farm Bureau, which led the opposition—although we did get support from some farm groups. We also got an impressive lineup of religious leaders to endorse the need for a grain reserve. But our main leverage again was the outpouring of letters to U.S. senators and representatives from our members, churches, and groups such as the Interreligious Task Force on U.S. Food Policy, and Network (led by Catholic nuns), which had became part of a growing coalition.

We faced the same problem we had with the *Right to Food Resolution*: strong support in Congress as a whole, but resistance from the agriculture committees. Terry Martin and I met with Senator Humphrey, who was eager to help. Humphrey and Senator George McGovern (D-SD) had previously introduced separate bills for more modest grain reserves without success. "Farmers," Humphrey told us, "are capitalists at the top and socialists at the bottom"—meaning they don't want government restrictions when prices are high, but seek government help when prices are low. He suggested that we bring some farmers from different parts of the country to Washington to testify before the Senate Agriculture Committee. We did so. We met in a fairly small room, with the committee seated around a large table. The farmers spoke with a down-to-earth authenticity that clearly got the ear of committee members. An amazing discussion followed unlike any other congressional hearing I have ever attended. Committee members began talking informally to one another about the issue, engaging the farmers from time to time. Humphrey and Senator Bob Dole (R-KS) began to exchange humorous quips that had everyone laughing. Within a few days after that friendly bipartisan hearing the committee approved the bill, and eventually so did the full Senate.

Once again the House proved to be more difficult. "Congress will not vote for a reserve," said Tom Foley, chairman of the House Committee on Agriculture, which rejected the bill by a 16-5 vote. But it was proposed on the floor of the House as an amendment to the farm bill and, after extended debate, approved.

Enactment of a 35-million-ton, farmer-owned grain reserve on August 29, 1977, was the second major victory in Congress for which Bread for the World's role was decisive. And a few months later, Martin

Tolchin, Capitol Hill reporter for *The New York Times*, cited Bread for the World as an example of an effective single-purpose lobby.

Seeking a Second Grain Reserve

In 1978 a PBS-TV affiliate in Pittsburgh asked Bread for the World to collaborate with them in the production of a three-part, three-hour documentary on world hunger entitled *The Fight for Food*. The producer, Al Perlmutter, consulted us regarding the shape and content of the program, which was broadcast nationally in November 1978. Bread was given a grant to produce discussion material on the program for mailing to tens of thousands of churches. This gave us another door to the churches and a golden opportunity to reach a wide audience. Julian Bond served as moderator for the documentary, part of which consisted of panel discussions on several topics, including one on Bread's new proposal for a 4-million-ton, emergency wheat reserve to be tapped for famine prevention. That gave us a chance on national television to state briefly the case for this additional reserve.

Bread for the World began working for a government-owned emergency reserve immediately after the farmer-owned reserve was signed into law by President Carter. Our hope of passing both reserves in one bill had failed when a parliamentary ruling separated them. The first reserve helped stabilize the price and supply of grain, but could not be expected to prevent famines or natural disasters that require emergency aid. A second reserve was needed for quick response to those emergencies.

Enactment of the initial farmer-owned reserve was warmly welcomed in international circles. But the global food crisis occurring at the time of the 1974 World Food Conference, and the lethargic U.S. response to the crisis, illustrated brilliantly why the emergency reserve was also necessary. In the face of famine, U.S. food aid had plummeted from more than 9 million tons of grain in 1972 to 3.3 million tons in 1974. Why? Because shortages caused the price of grain to soar, so the amount of money budgeted for food aid bought much less. This turned reality upside down. Opponents of the reserve argued that the government should pay for the grain when it was needed. But the problem was that when the need became most urgent, money allotted for that purpose bought much less. The Ford administration was also worried that additional purchases on the market would aggravate already-high inflation. As a result, we responded to starvation by reducing food aid, and then delayed for months until pressure built up for an extra appropriation while people died.

Bread for the World's campaign followed a predictable path, as letters and visits with members of Congress garnered strong support for the emergency reserve. But once again—no surprise—it met stiff resistance in the agriculture committees. Alan Grant of the Farm Bureau argued on the PBS *Fight for Food* panel that the reserve would penalize farmers, who could make more money if emergency food had to be purchased when prices were high—an argument in favor of starvation. Yet agriculture committee opposition kept the bill from being brought to the floor of either the House or the Senate for a vote. There it lay, receiving a slow burial.

Then a remarkable thing happened.

In December 1979 the Soviet Union invaded Afghanistan to rescue its tottering Soviet-supported Communist government. President Carter protested by announcing a U.S. boycott of the 1980 Olympics in Moscow and by placing an embargo on a shipment of 4 million tons of wheat to the Soviet Union. Suddenly the collapse of that wheat sale breathed new life into the proposed grain reserve. The U.S. government bought the wheat in order to avoid putting it on the market where the extra supply would have lowered the price of wheat and hurt farmers. Since the government already owned the 4 million tons of wheat, farmers decided it would be better to have wheat secured in a reserve with strict conditions on its use than to leave its use in doubt. So the main source of opposition to the reserve began to think more kindly of it.

Obstacles remained, but some members of Congress went out of their way to overcome them. Rep. Foley spoke forcefully in the House-Senate conference to get some of Bread's key provisions included, specifically referring to them as Bread's concerns. The agreement went to the full House and Senate for approval, and was signed into law by President Carter on December 3. The next day we had a celebration on Capitol Hill that included Secretary of Agriculture Bob Berglund and some of the bill's key backers in Congress, among them Matt McHugh (D-NY), one of the lead sponsors of the bill in the House. A couple of decades later he became chair of Bread's board of directors. A few weeks after the celebration I got a phone call from Berglund, who told me that The Food Security Wheat Reserve of 1980 would be in place before the January 20 inauguration of Ronald Reagan.

That was our third major victory. The reserve was later modified to include corn, rice, and sorghum. Still later, as part of *The Africa Seeds of Hope Act of 1998* (another Bread initiative), it was renamed the Bill Emerson Humanitarian Trust in honor of a Republican congressman who had worked faithfully as a member of the House Select Committee on Hunger on many of our issues. Between 1980 and 2006 the reserve was tapped a dozen times to provide more than 6-million metric tons of food. And in response to the global food crisis that is happening in 2008, as I write, the Bush administration has released another half-million tons of grain from the reserve. Over the years this reserve has given the equivalent of a nearly five-month supply of food to 100 million people. How many lives have been saved? How many others gained hope in the face of crippling circumstances? God alone knows. And the beneficiaries will never know about the link between their survival and messages to Congress written by a lot of Bread members and faithful church-goers—each letter, on average, extending a lifeline to hundreds of desperate people.

12

Hunger at Home

I am sometimes asked, "How many lobbyists does Bread for the World have?" My current answer is "61,000," because our *members* are the ones who contact decision makers on behalf of hungry people. They write letters, send e-mails, make phone calls, visit their U.S. senators and representatives, organize Bread chapters, influence others in the churches, alert newspaper editors and reporters to our issues, and contribute money to support all of this. They are the heartbeat of Bread and, above all others, deserve credit for its achievements because, without them, Bread would have died at birth. They also form the core of a far-reaching network of church bodies, local churches, charities, coalition partners, and influential persons who respect Bread's work, not to mention thousands of others who connect with Bread for the World electronically.

But I must immediately pay tribute to Bread's staff, on whom our members and this network depend, although I've mentioned only a few of them and all too briefly. Their dedication and diverse talents have kept Bread on the cutting edge of its work.

To members and staff alike, the choosing of policy targets is crucial. Not long after Bread for the World was up and running, we began developing criteria to guide us in the selection of issues and give us a consistent frame of reference against which to test possibilities. These criteria compel us to ask, among other things: Is a proposed target clearly a hunger issue? If it becomes U.S. policy, what difference might it be expected to make for hungry people? Is it an issue that the membership has been prepared to act on? Is it one that can be explained clearly? Would Bread's role be apt to make a significant difference in the outcome? Questions such as these guide us. The selection of issues evokes intense and sometimes heated discussion, because much is at stake and staff members feel deeply involved. The process is always informed by Bread members and activists whom we poll, as well as church leaders, coalition partners, and congressional offices. Recommendations ultimately come from the staff, and decisions are made by our board of directors. The process is not simple, but each year it helps us determine targets of opportunity on which Bread seems to have the best chance of helping hungry people.

Focus is essential. Effective work usually requires us to have only one major campaign each year, with more-limited effort possible on just a few other issues. However, even limited efforts may achieve an important outcome. In 1978 we got Congress to pass "human needs" legislation that required the U.S. representative to the International Monetary Fund to insist on steps to protect people affected by a special IMF lending facility to poor countries. It was a modest victory, noticed by few, but one that nudged the International Monetary Fund in the right direction. Another short but intense campaign spurred U.S. aid to famine-stricken Cambodia in 1979, following a reign of genocide. These focused efforts and others like them were of huge consequence to the families and individuals given a chance to live.

Hunger in the USA

Among the factors that we consider in our selection of issues is the balance between hunger abroad and hunger at home. From what I have written so far, it may seem to you that Bread for the World paid little attention to hunger in our own country. That was not the case then, nor is it now. We did focus heavily on global hunger in our earliest years, partly because hunger is far more extreme and widespread in poor countries, and partly because Bread was born during an international food crisis in 1974 when hunger in the United States seemed to be receding. Poverty had dropped from 22 to 13 percent of the population during Lyndon Johnson's administration and reached an all-time low of 11.1 percent under President Nixon in 1973.

Forces were at work, however, to reverse this favorable trend, and to our shame as a nation, we have yet to improve upon that 1973 achievement, despite massive economic growth during the intervening thirty-five years. Scrooge-like voices began to surface. Treasury Secretary William Simon called food stamps "a haven for chiselers and rip-off artists." Agriculture Secretary Earl Butz said, "Hunger is relative—if your larder is empty, you cut back some." (Cut back on empty?) And in the Senate, Democrat Herman Talmadge introduced a bill for the Ford administration that would have eliminated everyone above the poverty line from the food stamp program and compelled those below the poverty line to pay more for their food stamps—a payment requirement (no longer in force) that was already keeping many of the poorest people off the program.

We wanted to improve and expand nutrition programs, not gut them, because they prevent millions of Americans from going hungry, and could, if adequately funded, quickly eliminate most hunger in the nation. Such an investment in the health and well-being of our people would bring dividends to the entire nation. But hunger is largely invisible to most Americans, and hungry people have little political clout. As a result, efforts to cut nutrition programs have persisted over the years, and Bread for the World has frequently been forced to fight proposed cuts. Defending against cuts is not glamorous work, but without that work countless additional families would go hungry.

We have not been the only ones speaking out, of course. The Food Research Action Center, the Center on Budget and Policy Priorities, and Feeding America play large roles in alerting the public to the facts about hunger in the United States. But unless and until we enlist a critical mass of citizen advocates, millions of Americans will continue to find the larder empty with no way to cut back, despite our nation's wealth.

There are champions of the issue in Congress, to be sure. Perhaps the most prominent of these in our early years were Senators George McGovern (D-SD) and Bob Dole (R-KS), who became the backbone of the Senate Select Committee on Nutrition and Human Needs, and who often formed a bipartisan team in seeking to make the nation's nutrition programs more effective and available. McGovern tells of watching a CBS documentary on hunger, as a reporter asked a young schoolboy how it felt to be hungry while others were having lunch. The boy looked down and said quietly, "I'm embarrassed." McGovern was shocked. "That's terrible!" he said. "I am a member of Congress and I'm the one who ought to be embarrassed." He and Bob Dole (currently on our board of directors) began to lead efforts against hunger and are still doing so in retirement, as their book *Ending Hunger Now* amply demonstrates. The two of them are the 2008 recipients of the World Food prize for their leadership in promoting child nutrition programs worldwide, which build on the success of school lunch and breakfast programs in our own country.

Despite occasional deep cuts in U.S. nutrition programs, Bread for the World has had more success than failure in helping to expand and improve them over the years. The requirement that recipients had to pay for food stamps, for example, was eliminated. Fraud—never as extensive as reports often asserted—has been reduced to near zero. But the food stamp program still does not enable recipients to buy *enough* food, including fruits and vegetables, not just cheap calories. The application process that confuses and intimidates people has been improved, along with outreach to eligible people not receiving help. Yet in 2008, while 31 million Americans received benefits from the food stamp program, 11 million others who qualified received none.

The Supplemental Nutrition Program for Women, Infants, and Children (WIC) began nationwide in 1974 to assist pregnant women and children up to age five who are certified to be in need both financially and physically. The WIC program provides packages of food that provide nutrients typically lacking in their diets, along with nutrition education and referrals to health care. Studies indicate that this assistance saves the public money, because it reduces health care costs, especially for emergencies among premature infants. As a result, it has attracted strong bipartisan support. Bread for the World's efforts have played a big part in bringing this about. Bread has campaigned hard and successfully to extend the program's coverage to about 60 percent of those eligible, arguably among our most notable achievements. By 2008 that threw a lifeline to more than 8 million women and children at a cost of more than $5 billion. The nutrition program has significantly reduced hunger among pregnant women and little children, prevented many premature deaths, and reduced child mortality in the United States. But there is still not adequate funding to reach the rest who qualify.

As early as 1979, Bread's Offering of Letters campaign urged annual national surveys to determine the extent of hunger in the

United States. We highlighted the need for such data and kept hammering away at it, largely because of policy analyst Barbara Howell's persistence—an essential virtue in the struggle to end hunger. Many who argued that hunger was not much of a problem and who said evidence for it was based on anecdotes, not reliable sampling, were strangely opposed to reliable sampling. It was not until 1995 that such a system was finally put in place and the Census Bureau began doing large-scale, random, scientifically valid interviews throughout the country, on the basis of which the U.S. Department of Agriculture began issuing annual reports. That at least gives people a more accurate picture of hunger in this country. Sometimes an accurate picture prods the nation's conscience enough to stimulate action.

Meanwhile, local Bread chapters and other groups did valuable nutrition surveys on a small scale. These indicated that millions of Americans, a large percentage of them children, were undernourished, and eventually the national surveys confirmed this. In 2007, 36 million Americans were found to have "food insecurity," with 12 million of these facing "very low food security." By this time, however, the administration had decided to replace the word *hunger* with *very low food security*. The terminology was more soothing to the public, but "very low food secure" people were still hungry. Others "merely" lived on the edge of hunger, going occasionally without food.

Bread also sought welfare reforms, which failed, and for a while we pushed hard in support of a full-employment bill (Humphrey-Hawkins), which passed in watered-down form. Bread's work made little difference on either of these issues beyond raising awareness. Full employment was important to us, because we saw jobs and income as the more enduring way out of hunger and poverty. Just as we stressed self-help development abroad, so we wanted to stress it at home as well. But we found it harder for Bread to influence such change in our own country than similar changes in poor countries. On an issue like employment in the United States, we are small players on a field that attracts many large and powerful interests, so our role is less likely to make a difference.

There was an exception to that in 1986. Bread for the World had a large hand in expanding the Earned Income Tax Credit (EITC), which rewards working poor people by reducing their taxes and sometimes adding a wage subsidy. Its expansion, part of a major overhaul of U.S. tax policy, led to 6 million low-income tax payers being removed from the tax rolls. "Bread for the World guided us through this effort and worked diligently with us to preserve the benefits for the poor in our [tax] bill....My Senate colleagues felt the presence of your strong grassroots organization," wrote Bob Packwood, chair of the Senate Finance Committee, in also praising Bread's policy analyst Fred Hutchinson, who worked closely with the committee staff and others on the bill. President Reagan applauded the tax bill as "the best anti-poverty, the best pro-family, the best job creation measure to come out of Congress." Bread supported an even larger expansion of EITC early in Bill Clinton's presidency, and by 2006 it added almost $2,000 a year to each of more than 22 million low-income tax filers, lifted more than 4 million of them above the poverty line, and gave a boost to many others who, even with EITC tax credits, still fell below the poverty line. The EITC deserves further expansion.

These programs and statistics may seem so remote from your life as to induce an afternoon nap. But, believe me, to kids who are forced to skip meals, or to a mother battling the odds to nourish them, or to a man working for a wage that forces his family to choose between heat or food, medicine or food, clothes or food—what I write about is the difference between desperation and hope. It is a matter of human decency on our part to tilt the arrangement toward hope.

13

Moving to Washington

I need to tell you about the Bread for the World Institute, which played a significant part in our early growth and development, as it does today. Because Bread for the World, as a registered lobby, cannot receive tax-deductible contributions, in 1975 we separately incorporated Bread for the World Institute as a sister agency that can receive such gifts for policy analysis and education on hunger. That gives us an extra stream of income, mostly from large donors and foundations.

In its earlier years, the Institute (or Educational Fund, as it was initially called) concentrated most of its work on holding seminars around the country. These attracted new members and trained participants to assume active roles as citizen advocates for hungry people. The Institute also did research that resulted in a wide range of studies, reports, and recommendations, as well as courses and worship aids. Since 1990 it is probably best known for its annual report on world hunger—an attractive, multicolor volume that focuses on a different theme each year and is used to some extent internationally by people engaged in reducing hunger and poverty. Research on key issues, such as those featured in the Institute's annual report on hunger, often plow the ground for subsequent legislative campaigns. For example, the Institute did a series of reports on different aspects of U.S. food-and-farm policy, preparing Bread for the World's members and the churches to campaign for broad reform of the 2007 farm bill. Institute analysts have also worked effectively for reforms of the World Bank and, more recently, of the U.S. food aid program.

The Institute's first major project was a "Decade of Commitment on World Hunger." Project conferences were aimed at the academic community—students, faculty, and campus ministries. The second big project was a series of seven regional gatherings on the report of President Carter's Commission on World Hunger. These in turn led to dozens of local public forums and hundreds of local study groups. From 1982 through 1985 the Institute held a series of thirty-seven "Outreach on Hunger" leadership training events in various states and regions. A cluster of "Beyond Charity" seminars followed. These events equipped thousands of hunger activists to use their influence as citizens, many for the first time, and many in leadership roles.

In recent years the Institute has spawned the Alliance to End Hunger, which I will say more about in chapter 17.

Traveling for Bread

In the beginning, Bread for the World grew at the rate of more than 5,000 new members a year, and by the end of 1980 we had 36,044 contributing members. We continued to grow during the 1980s, but at a slower pace. As we grew, so did my traveling and speaking schedule, which eventually took me to almost every state in the Union. Local Bread volunteers lined up media interviews and arranged public events. One of the great joys of my work with Bread was to meet people from various churches who trust the same Lord, know his saving love, and want to extend his love and justice to hungry people.

A Sunday-morning visit to the Bruderhof community in Rifton, New York, gave me one of my biggest surprises. I was sitting with about 250 simply dressed adults gathered quietly in concentric circles in a plain auditorium for worship. Suddenly, in unaccompanied four-part harmony, the entire congregation began singing Bach's "Break Forth, O Beauteous Heavenly Light." I felt I had been transported to heaven and placed in the midst of an angelic choir—which it was. On my next visit they sang the "Hallelujah Chorus" from Handel's *Messiah*.

Before leaving for a few weeks of speaking in the Los Angeles area, I glanced through our membership printout for names I recognized. I came across Jerry Voorhis. I wrote him a letter asking, "Are you by any chance the former congressman who was defeated by Richard Nixon?" Voorhis wrote back and said that he was, so I visited him at his home in Claremont. He was a gracious man and a devout

Methodist, and cared for an invalid wife. We had a fascinating conversation in which he told me how crushed he had felt about losing the election after being labeled a Communist sympathizer. "But you know," he said, "it was the best thing that ever happened to me, because I was asked to head the Cooperative League of the USA, and I spent the next two decades working for a great cause with the most wonderful people in the world." He gave me an autographed copy of his book *The Strange Case of Richard Milhaus Nixon*. I left thinking to myself, Who really lost that election, and who really won?

A few years later I was having lunch with Wally Campbell, who as an executive of the Cooperative League had helped to found CARE (Cooperative For Assistance and Relief Everywhere), and eventually retired as its president. He and Voorhis were good friends, so I asked him how Jerry was doing. "Not good," he said. "You should send him a note. His wife is sinking and he has to help her do everything." So I wrote, and he replied, "Yes, Wally's report is *sadly* quite correct. My dear, dear wife of fifty-eight years married has quite lost her mental way. She is still very sweet and dear with me and I love her—if such is possible—more than ever." I was deeply moved. (He added a P.S. "Your brother is still my very favorite congressman.") A few years later I got a note from his granddaughter Victoria, who had been a member of Bread for some time, and she said that her grandfather's membership gift had brought her into Bread for the World.

Another unexpected bonus of leading Bread was the chance to visit people and places in poor countries. Bread operated on such a tight budget that I never traveled abroad on its money, though I should have because of its value to Bread. Instead I "hitchhiked" abroad from time to time on invitations from others. My first such opportunity came in 1979 when Paul McCleary, director of Church World Service, asked me to accompany two of his staff members, Doug Beane and Bill Herod, to Vietnam. Doug and Bill had worked many years there for Church World Service and knew both the country and its language well. We traveled north and south, among the earliest Americans to do so after the war. It was an eye-opening introduction to a very poor country. The Vietnamese were almost uniformly thin. Vietnam was experiencing severe food shortages, and extreme poverty was evident everywhere. So was their determination. They made something out of every scrap we normally discard—

117

string, tin cans, strips of cloth. Sandals made from old tires were especially popular. I took a picture of a man in Hanoi looking into a mostly empty store window of a government department store. His shirt was so threadbare that parts of it were held together by wire.

We visited a new economic zone, where farms and villages were being carved out of the jungle. In Hanoi, the capital, each household was allowed one 15-watt light bulb, and families were crowded into tiny old apartments. We had dinner with the mayor of Hanoi who told us, when I asked, that he and his wife lived with a daughter, her husband, and their small child in a two-room apartment that also had one 15-watt bulb. These things have given me a much different perspective on our wasteful use of energy and the piling up of luxuries that characterizes our culture. Why should we have so much when others have so little?

Although I think the mayor was being truthful, I learned not to take at face value everything we were told, because the party line prevailed on topics such as the Chinese invasion of a northern province of Vietnam a few months earlier. Officials repeatedly told us that there were no Vietnamese but thousands of Chinese casualties. Implausible! We visited the provincial capital and saw vast destruction that must have taken many Vietnamese lives. Officials knew, and they must have known that we knew, but they still repeated the obligatory party line with a straight face.

In Thailand I visited a refugee camp for Cambodians who had survived Cambodia's genocide, and another camp for Laotians who had risked their lives crossing the Mekong River to gain freedom. Then in India, I saw some of the work being done in Calcutta by Mother Teresa's Missionaries of Charity—the House of the Dying, where men, rescued from the street, are allowed to die in loving hands; a place for children, where abandoned infants (almost all of them girls) are cared for until homes are found; a village with residential and outpatient care for lepers, and much more. I learned that the Calcutta Metropolitan Development Authority, which I visited, gave Mother Teresa credit for changing fatalistic attitudes toward suffering and giving people of Calcutta a sense of hope.

I spent some days in rural villages of India, where tribal people, assisted by the Lutheran World Federation, had started tiny cottage industries and were turning barren land into small productive plots by building irrigation systems. Next to one village was a large reservoir that villagers had dug with hand tools as part of a food-for-work aid project. Villagers spoke of a nearby landowner who owned more land than was legally permitted and who also served as the local money lender. By promising water, he tried to discourage them from digging the reservoir. They all owed him money. I asked how much interest he charged, and they cited bags of rice and days of labor that translated into annual interest rates ranging from 200 to 300 percent. Digging that reservoir and bringing barren land into production was a way to freedom from the money lender, better nutrition, and the easing of their poverty. In the process they were also developing self-confidence and a stronger sense of community.

Subsequent trips included ones to West Africa with Church World Service; the Philippines with the Community of Christ; East Africa with World Vision; Brazil with the International Fund for Agricultural Development; and Ecuador, Uganda, and Kenya with Christian Children's Fund. Each trip was a treasured opportunity, a chance to be with people for whom hunger and poverty are not abstractions but part of their daily struggle. The invitation to East Africa from World Vision came in 1984 as famines were emerging in Ethiopia and other countries. Bob Ainsworth, president of World Vision Relief, had visited the U.S. Agency for International Development, and afterward dropped in unannounced to my office to report that wherever he turned, the agency's staff members told him that Bread for the World had built a fire of public support for famine relief, and this had prompted a faster and larger U.S. response. It also gave us stronger ties to World Vision.

Aid for Self-Reliance

Bread for the World began at a time when U.S. humanitarian and development aid for poor countries was declining. We wanted to stop the decline and reverse it. We also saw that assistance needed to be greatly improved. Much of it was shaped by political considerations driven by the Cold War. And much of it was still captive to the theory that if we stimulated economic growth, the benefits would automatically trickle down to poor people, although the evidence showed not nearly enough trickled down.

From the outset we recognized the huge role that private enterprise plays in historic gains against hunger and poverty, but we also knew that the free market leaves many people struggling to survive, and we saw aid as a way of creating opportunities for them. So we worked to direct more assistance to poor people, especially the kind of assistance that enables them to thrive without depending on further assistance—exactly what poor people want most. Joe Short, director of Oxfam-America, told me of watching a shipment of aid to Cambodia arrive in 1979, after genocide had wiped out two million Cambodians and left others starving. Bags of food were unloaded onto the dock and a crowd of Cambodians clapped politely in appreciation. But when fishing nets were unloaded the people cheered.

Bread worked hard for swift and generous aid to Cambodia, but we also began a broader campaign, *Aid for Self-Reliance*. We were especially keen on making sure that our food assistance did not undermine the livelihood of local farmers by making food too cheap, or create an unnecessary dependency on food aid, and in either case have the long-term effect of causing more hunger. We considered increased food production by struggling farmers in poor countries to be the main solution. Year after year we helped tailor legislation along those lines. Congress often approved with small steps in the right direction, but we swam against a powerful political tide of receding foreign aid. That tide, along with an astonishingly shortsighted neglect of agriculture by donor and recipient nations, paved the way for future hunger crises, especially in Africa. As I write, both aid-giving and aid-receiving governments are scrambling to strengthen agriculture in poor countries because of soaring food prices and the resulting setback in the world's progress against hunger.

From Bread's earliest days we were also concerned about the relationship between military spending and hunger. Attending our January 1976 board meeting was Norman Borlaug, who is considered "the father of the Green Revolution" for his role in the development of high-yielding corn and wheat that did much to keep food production ahead of population growth. Borlaug held up the front page of *The New York Times*. Its headlines reported that for the first time the president was proposing a defense budget of more than $100 billion dollars. "That's the problem," he said. "Too much for the military and not enough to help farmers in poor countries produce more food." But defense spending continued to rise, so Bread crafted legislation that was introduced in 1981 as the *Hunger and Global Security* bill. It featured the Carter commission's major recommendation: that the United States make the elimination of hunger the primary focus of its relationships with developing countries. It stressed that major initiatives against hunger would strengthen U.S. and global security. It proposed shifting U.S. aid toward the poorest families, and giving trade concessions to the poorest countries. The main purpose of the bill was to change the way policy makers think about hunger and about security. It helped to do that—and some of its specific reforms were approved—but we could not get Congress to enact the Carter commission's main recommendation.

The following year we struggled to get Congress to require that at least 50 percent of U.S. development assistance would benefit primarily people classified by the World Bank as living in "absolute poverty," which usually entails chronic hunger. The Reagan administration fought against this, while letters built congressional support for it. In the end a compromise reduced the requirement to 40 percent and applied it to only one year, but it was still hotly contested—so much so that the administrator of the U.S. Agency for International Development took the unusual step of personally buttonholing members of Congress outside the doors of the House chamber to urge its defeat. It passed anyway. One unexpected benefit was that, for the first time, I got a call from the agency's administrator, Peter McPherson, inviting me to meet with him and talk about ways in which we could work together. Ernie Loevinsohn, our policy analyst on this issue, and I met twice with him, and we felt that, within the constraints of the Reagan administration, he probably bent toward us as much as he could. Ernie later became the staff director of the House Select Committee on Hunger, and is currently director general for health and nutrition of the Canadian International Development Agency. McPherson went on to head Michigan State University and has worked closely with Bread for the World in advocacy for increased agricultural development assistance.

Relocations

Two big changes occurred during the early 1980s, one very personal to me, and the other to the entire Bread staff. What hit me hard personally was a decision by my wife Kaiya to end our marriage. The change that affected the whole staff was a decision to relocate our headquarters from New York to the nation's capital in Washington. Each of these happened while Bread was growing rapidly and tackling new initiatives.

The hardest part of writing this book has to do with Kaiya's decision to leave the marriage in 1981. She left the Christian faith and began thinking in a very different way about a lot of things, quite unhappy that I was unwilling to change with her. In the end she said she needed out of the marrigage.

I was dismayed. The crisis compelled me to take a closer look at myself. I had been too busy with Bread, not attentive enough to our family, taking too much for granted—common failings of husbands, but deplorable all the same. I was pained most of all to think what this would mean for our sons, then ten and eight years old. The very worst and saddest moment of my life was when we broke the news to Nathan and Peter. They sobbed and ran around the apartment screaming, "No! No! No! I don't want you to do that! I don't want this to happen!" We had just handed them the collapse of their childhood. All that they had trusted and depended on was crumbling before their eyes. No more meals together, no more family outings, no more evenings at home or strolls down the street, no more Christmas around the tree for all of us, no more *anything* together. The family, the nest they knew and cherished and depended on, was finished. And they were helpless to do anything about it.

I knew this would leave scars, but the reality was far worse than I imagined. So please do not tell me that marriage vows are "only" a covenant between husband and wife. They are also a promise to children, a promise to give them the love and security of a family that will undergird them for life. We had robbed Nathan and Peter of that and they suffered for it. Our once-happy family had become another sign of the world's brokenness.

Board and staff members were very understanding. Neuhaus invited me occasionally for dinner, and Gene Blake sent me one of the most gracious letters I've ever received. To my shame, however, I carried a resentment for years before realizing that I had been unwilling to forgive—or, for that matter, unwilling to acknowledge to myself and God that my own shortcomings also contributed to the breakdown of the marriage. As I have written elsewhere, the Lord's Prayer played a big role in my own healing, and the healing continues.

That change affected me. The relocation of our headquarters from New York to Washington affected the entire staff.

Moving our headquarters was nothing new. We started with a couple of rooms in my church's parish house. Several months after launching nationally, we moved to New York Theological Seminary in midtown Manhattan. A year and a half later the seminary sold the building, so we found quarters in the parish building of St. George's Episcopal Church on East 16th Street. In three years we outgrew that and rented the fourth floor of an old building facing Union Square. It was barren warehouse space, but it served our purpose. So we painted the walls and moved in.

The move to Washington was an entirely different matter. By all logic, Bread's office belonged in the nation's capital from the start, but those of us who founded Bread lived in New York and we had no money to consider starting anywhere else. Our Washington-based policy analyst, Barbara Howell, found a bit of space for us to use as a "branch office," located in the Methodist Building across the street from the Capitol Building. But our other policy analysts often had to travel at night by train to or from Washington, because much of their work, and occasionally mine, involved meeting with congressional staff members and other policy shapers. Even with a couple of mattresses for overnight travelers, this arrangement imposed a hardship on policy analysts, who already had heavy work loads.

The arrangement had its lighter moments as well. Once when arriving late at night, at the door of the building I found a forgotten briefcase with gold lettering: "Albert Gore, Sr." Gore, a retired U.S. senator from Tennessee, had an apartment in the same building. The next morning I gave the briefcase to his son, Al Gore, Jr., a brand new member of the House. I also gave him a little speech about Bread for the World that seemed to draw a puzzled look. I had that particular gift.

On another occasion Lane Vanderslice, a new Bread policy analyst, was sitting on the steps of the front door of the building one summer evening, waiting for someone to come and open the door because he had forgotten his key. Along came Senator Patrick Leahy of Vermont, who years later joined our board. Lane felt he ought to do something as a U.S. senator walked by, so he yelled out, "You're doing a great job, Senator!" And Leahy yelled back, "Thanks! I needed that. It's been a rough day."

As Bread and its staff grew larger and more deeply engaged with policy makers, the burden increased, and so did the pressure to relocate. Doing so met with resistance on the part of staff members who could not or did not want to consider moving to Washington. One of them argued (in all seriousness) that the hardship on our policy analysts was good, because it kept them humble. Others more thoughtfully worried that Bread might lose its emphasis on advocacy by our members and would become another victim of "the DC syndrome"—inside-the-beltway thinking that loses touch with the rest of the country. We took that concern seriously.

By this time we had a staff of forty-two, but moving to Washington meant losing and finding replacements for fifteen of these, including my executive assistant, Mary Good, whose name describes her perfectly. I thought her irreplaceable until Dolly Youssef from Bloomington, Indiana, applied. The two of them were the best of the best, handling people and documents with remarkable skill and helping me organize my work and facilitate that of the board and staff. They served throughout my years at Bread, and Dolly continues to do so. Each has made an extraordinary behind-the-scenes contribution to Bread's mission.

In July 1982, following a long search for space, we moved our headquarters to a basement warehouse at the edge of Washington, not a good location, but affordable. A year later we signed a 10-year lease for space in an old building just one Metro train stop from Capitol Hill. It required painting, and more used furniture, but we were getting closer to where we belonged. In 2000 Bread was finally able to relocate to Capitol Hill.

In June of 1984 I married Rosamund James, whose son Richard became part of our new family. Two years after that, our daughter Leah was born, the joy of my seasoned years.

14

Setbacks and Successes

In 1983 we began getting reports of a serious food shortage in Ethiopia, which was gradually turning into a catastrophic regional famine, so we began to campaign for emergency U.S. aid. We got there well ahead of the national media, which had not yet given coverage to the famine. In addition to alerting members, we convened a national one-day summit on the African crisis that drew representatives from forty-seven church-related agencies. We later did a media blitz in thirty cities, led by our new media specialist, Cureton Johnson. The public response to these efforts prompted Congress and the administration to move more quickly with increased U.S. assistance.

Things were going well, and for more than a year the board had urged me to take a sabbatical. So from February through June of 1985, I wrote *Christian Faith and Public Policy*,* which makes the case for citizen action against hunger. The book addressed a tough challenge that Bread for the World constantly faces: persuading Christians that seeking justice for hungry people is both biblically faithful and effective. The book was timely because of the sudden entrance of many fundamentalists into the political arena, as represented especially by Jerry Falwell and his organization, the Moral Majority. Think of Pat Robertson's metamorphosis: In 1975, when he interviewed me on the *700 Club* broadcast, he disparaged the role of government. In 1988, he ran as a presidential candidate in the primaries.

The problem, as I saw it, was not the welcome discovery of the "religious right" that Christians have a responsibility to let their light shine in the political arena. The problem was their connecting a right-wing political ideology to the Bible. The religious right used the media

---

* Arthur Simon, *Christian Faith and Public Policy* (Grand Rapids, MI: Eerdmans Publishing Co., 1987).

effectively in attracting a large following and managed to become a powerful faction within the Republican Party, but in the process they debased the meaning of *Christian* and *evangelical* for many people.

I got a personal taste of this during the 1984 U.S. senate campaign in Illinois, when my brother Paul was successfully challenging Senator Charles Percy. The Christian Voice, a political entity with links to the Moral Majority, gave Paul a zero rating on his voting record because of such "anti-Christian" things as supporting the establishment of a federal department of education, and sponsoring a bill to protect women against spouse abuse. I was at O'Hare airport in Chicago on my way to Washington, when, among those waiting for a flight, I noticed the familiar face of Lyn Nofziger, political advisor to President Reagan, who was running for reelection. I had just read Mike Royko's column in *The Chicago Tribune* that morning, which poked fun at the Christian Voice for giving Paul a zero rating. I showed the column to Nofziger. He read it and laughed, saying he thought the zero rating would backfire and help Paul in the election. To my surprise Nofziger added that it would please him to see Paul win, though I think that had to do more with his displeasure at Percy as a moderate Republican than with enthusiasm for Paul.

I returned from my sabbatical to some highly encouraging developments. Bread's work on Africa was paying off in several ways. We had seen large and timely increases in famine assistance. Our campaign to secure passage of the $800 million *African Relief and Recovery Act of 1985*, which we had helped to craft, was gaining momentum in Congress and on its way toward passage. And our membership was rising to record levels—48,655 by the end of 1985. Though all of this pleased us, none of it came as a surprise, and based on the expectation of continued growth we expanded our operations.

Soon, however, a dark cloud on the horizon began to alarm us: growth in income was lagging unexpectedly behind our expenses. Past successes had given us unwarranted confidence. For more than a decade we experienced continued growth and allowed for little margin of error, typically borrowing during the summer and ending the year just barely in the black. Almost a third of our annual income came during the last two months of the year, enough to erase deficits. In 1985, however, for the first time the deficit threatened to spin out of control despite success on other fronts. But why?

We had underestimated the impact of a sluggish economy from which other nonprofit organizations were also suffering. In addition we found that many of our members and donors who normally gave special contributions to Bread were instead channeling their gifts to private relief agencies in response to the famine, partly because of our own encouragement. Having gotten the government to do its part, they now wanted to help famine victims by giving private agencies a boost. We failed to anticipate this.

The money crunch dismayed us because we had hired additional staff. Now it was necessary to make cuts. Few things during my years at Bread for the World were more painful than having to let several staff members go and curtail new initiatives. The shortfall prompted the board to send a special financial appeal to the members and to increase basic membership from $15 to $25 a year. These moves erased our deficit in less than two months and put us on solid financial footing again—but at a high cost.

The cost was a drop in membership, our first ever. A few years earlier we had raised the membership from $10 to $15 to catch up with inflation, but we had warned members in advance that the increase would occur and allowed them to renew at the old rate one more time, if they chose to do so. The new increase, however, was abrupt and steep. In addition, many of the new members we had attracted in 1985 were responding to the emergency in Africa and had no interest in advocating for hungry people on other issues, so they failed to renew their membership. As a result, our membership plummeted by almost 9,000 during 1986, after which it began growing again, but slowly. Fortunately the drop in numbers did not seem to affect the commitment of the members who stayed and continued to advocate faithfully for hungry people.

Our financial woes forced us to put a hold on staff sabbaticals, except for three already under way. Joel Underwood took one of these for the purpose of writing a musical. The result, I am happy to say, was a delightful hit, named *Lazarus*. Based on the parable of the rich man and Lazarus in Luke 16, its music and lyrics have captivated audiences in hundreds of performances around the country, mostly by local groups.

Broadening the Movement

As Bread for the World grew, it became increasingly clear that, while we were well integrated by gender and church denomination, that was not the case regarding people of color. The reasons for this did not include lack of trying. For one thing, we *looked* too much like a white organization. For another, bitter experience over several centuries taught African Americans to doubt that their appeals to government officials would likely change anything. Also, the civil rights movement attuned many to forms of direct action more visible than letter-writing. In addition, their leaders were typically overloaded with immediate hands-on efforts to deal with poverty problems. At any rate, only 2 percent of our membership could be identified as African American, despite the fact that our work disproportionately benefits Africans and African Americans. A similar pattern prevailed regarding Latinos, though by sustained effort we now have substantially higher percentages from both groups.

We did better on staff, with a rigorous equal employment policy, but the pool of qualified African Americans for various professional positions was (again for historical reasons) limited, competition for them was keen, and our salaries were usually below the market level.

In the early 1980s we set out on a long-range "Broadening the Movement" effort. This included workshops for the staff as well as members at conferences and at our national gatherings. I should have taken a more direct hand in shaping these. I think they worked well when we brought in consultants who could help us deal with issues of prejudice and inclusion on the basis of our equality in Christ. That empowered and united us. But racial awareness efforts that stressed confrontation and set up an accuser/accused dynamic tended to discourage and separate people.

We worked in a variety of ways to recruit more members among racial and ethnic minorities. And we let the members know, loud and clear, mainly through our newsletter, that we wanted to "broaden the movement" and become more racially inclusive. Sometimes we may have been too loud. At one point, to the distress of some staff members, I pulled a newsletter background paper that I felt was breast-beating and guilt-inducing. So we struggled as a staff to get this right. Arnold Graf of the Industrial Areas Foundation offered pro bono help—his own and especially that of one of his most skilled organizers, Gerald Taylor, an African American—to evaluate our situation and make recommendations. Taylor concluded that if racial diversity were not subordinated to Bread's central mission, we would undermine that mission and do a disservice to African Americans and others, despite good intentions. It was a needed corrective that helped to unite the staff as we continued to broaden the movement but in less strained ways.

We have outstanding people of color on our staff, our board, and in our membership. David Beckmann, my successor at Bread, has shown strong leadership in helping us become more inclusive. Sharon Pauling, who started as our office and personnel manager, grew so knowledgeable that she became a policy analyst specializing in Africa, and after many years with us was hired by the U.S. Agency for International Development. For more than two decades, another staff member, Bishop Donald Williams, has opened door after door for us among historically African American denominations. Bread is now making similar efforts to reach more Latinos.

The Reagan Years

Each presidency and the makeup of each Congress greatly affects Bread for the World. We have always worked in a nonpartisan fashion, eager to cooperate with both parties, but not hesitating to challenge them either. The 1980s were clearly the decade of President Ronald Reagan. We sometimes had to defend U.S. nutrition and international aid programs during the Ford and Carter administrations because of budget pressures, but the Reagan administration was exceptionally hard on poor people, repeatedly and often successfully seeking cuts in antipoverty programs. That made our work much more difficult.

Military spending and military aid rose to new heights, large tax breaks benefited mainly the well-to-do, and the nation's annual deficit soared to record levels. All of this put pressure on reducing costs elsewhere, and Reagan's first budget proposed $41 billion in cuts. The "truly needy" should bear no share of this, he said, but antipoverty programs provided the softest political target, so his budget sought a nearly 40 percent cut in child nutrition, 15 percent in food stamps, and 26 percent in foreign aid. Despite our best efforts, during Reagan's first year in office one million people were removed from the food stamp program and its benefits were reduced for others.

The administration proposed more deep cuts in subsequent years. Reagan himself seems to have disconnected his personal compassion from government policy. He was said to be willing to give a man the shirt off his back, but signed legislation that took food away from his family. Come to think of it, that seems a lot like people who contribute food for hungry people to a local pantry but remain silent while Congress takes food from millions of them, or perhaps simply neglects them. This disconnection is epidemic even in our churches, an example of what theologian Reinhold Niebuhr called "moral man and immoral society"—the combining of personal virtue with action or inaction that causes collective injustice. It continues to be a major obstacle to the ending of hunger.

The Reagan years compelled Bread to fight defensive battles. But, as they say, the best defense is a good offense, so we took the initiative, sometimes achieving reforms and restorations, but more often blunting the impact of destructive cuts, especially for nutrition programs in this country. In 1983 Bread for the World helped to draft the *Preventing Hunger at Home* resolution and campaigned successfully with others to get Congress to pass it. That put the brakes on cuts for a year. By the end of Reagan's presidency we had battled the administration to a near draw. Adjusted for inflation, funding for domestic food programs dropped by five percent. But campaigns to expand the Women, Infants, and Children nutrition program nearly doubled the number participating in it. Bread also played an important part in obtaining tax breaks for millions of working poor people through the Earned Income Tax Credit (EITC; see chapter 12). The EITC and the nutrition program stand out as exceptions to the trend during the 1980s to shift income away from the poor to the prosperous. To Reagan's credit, he approved of the EITC.

With millions of additional Americans desperate to put food on the table during the 1980s, food banks, food pantries, and soup kitchens grew by leaps and bounds. As essential as these efforts are, however, they may reflect the failure of public justice as much as the triumph of charity. Their outreach is limited, and they cannot possibly make up for gaps and deficiencies in the food stamp and other nutrition programs. They serve as a short-term safety net of last resort, not as a substitute for national responsibility.

The 1980s were a lost decade for many of the world's poor. As U.S. military aid doubled, development assistance to poor countries sputtered, and the spending of poorest countries decreased by 25 percent on health care and 50 percent on education. In our own country, childhood poverty grew by 21 percent.

Agriculture and Microenterprise

Despite financial woes, Bread continued to work on a number of critical issues. One aimed at stimulating food production, and another promoted small enterprise in developing countries. Each sheds light on our understanding of effective aid.

Consider food production. Among all the recommendations of the 1974 World Food Conference, the most appallingly neglected was the expansion of food production by small-scale farmers in poor countries. For this purpose, the conference proposed an International Fund for Agricultural Development (IFAD) and recommended an annual budget of $5 billion—worth about $20 billion in 2007 dollars. IFAD was established, but funding never remotely approached the proposed level. Worse yet, between 1971 and 2004, the share of international aid designated for agriculture fell from 18 percent to 3.5 percent. This bias against agriculture also occurred within developing countries, despite the fact that the 450 million families who farm less than five acres make up the main part of the economy of the poorest countries and include a majority of the world's poorest people. Poor countries with economies based on agriculture (including most of Africa) spent about 10 percent of their budgets on agriculture in 1980, but by 2004 that had fallen to 4 percent, even though most of their people work in agriculture. It would be hard to invent a better way to perpetuate hunger.

With this concern in mind, Bread fought to increase U.S. support for IFAD. For less than the cost of sending a ton of emergency food to

Africa, IFAD enables a subsistence-level farm family to produce an additional ton of food annually for the rest of their lives, a clear indication of where the emphasis should—but regrettably does not—lie. In the mid-1980s the fund's survival was threatened when the administration balked for two years at an aid-funding ratio for IFAD between Western donor nations and oil-producing countries. Bread worked hard to keep IFAD alive and well, thanks in part to policy analyst John Tucker and our members who generated support in Congress from the voters back home. Even so, U.S. and international funding for it has lagged over the years; the funding gave IFAD a budget of $600 million in 2007, a mere 3 percent of the amount urged by the World Food Conference.

As Bread sought help for small-scale farmers, we also wanted to help small-scale entrepreneurs. So Bread gave strong support for including microenterprise in our foreign aid, although a coalition partner, Results, took the lead on this. The purpose of microenterprise is to enable very poor people—usually women—to start or expand a livelihood by receiving small-scale loans. They might buy chickens and sell eggs, buy an oven for baking and sell bread, open a tiny store, get tools for repairing bicycles, or maybe expand a small business and hire workers. I have seen the life-changing fruit of this many times. One mother in Kenya was so grateful for her flock of chickens that she gave me an entire day's supply of eggs, which I accepted in order not to offend her, but later asked if she would use them for me.

In 2006 Muhammad Yunus, founder of the Grameen Bank in Bangladesh, won the Nobel Peace Prize for his success in helping more than seven million impoverished women earn income through loans for enterprise. Women form small solidarity groups that monitor each other for timely payments, because a default by any one of them means the others in the group cannot receive further loans. This mix of personal responsibility and teamwork has resulted in a 98 percent rate of repayment. The Grameen Bank and countless similar groups give families a chance to have better health care, nourishment, and education for their children. They also gain a sense of hope and empowerment.

Rep. Tony Hall (D-OH), who became chair of the House Select Committee on Hunger when Rep. Mickey Leland (D-TX) was killed in a plane crash in Ethiopia, played an active role in promoting microenterprise, as he did for a wide range of antihunger initiatives. Tony, who later became U.S. ambassador to the UN food agencies and now serves on our board of directors, made hunger his primary concern and fought doggedly for more effective policies. At one point he fasted on a water-only diet for twenty-two days to protest congressional neglect. Bread worked actively to get the hunger committee established in 1984, and for a decade it generated support in Congress for many initiatives despite a lot of resistance and indifference.

Child Survival

Even during the politically difficult 1980s, breakthroughs occurred. One of these addressed the massive deaths among children in poor countries. The United Nations Children's Fund (UNICEF) and the World Health Organization launched a "Children's Health Revolution," which promoted the use of four simple, inexpensive methods that can greatly reduce the high mortality rate among infants and young children in poor countries: (1) breast-feeding, (2) the use of growth charts to catch problems before they become life-threatening, (3) immunization, and (4) oral rehydration—the use of the right combination of sugar, salt, and safe water to enable youngsters with diarrhea to retain fluid. (Micronutrients have since been added to the list.) The United Nations estimated that 40,000 young children from infancy to age five died *each day* from malnutrition and from diseases often related to malnutrition. That's the equivalent of a hundred jumbo jets, each holding 400 young children, crashing to the earth and leaving no survivors—one such crash every fourteen minutes.

Working with Reps. Tony Hall and Ben Gilman (R-NY), Bread policy analyst Lane Vanderslice crafted legislation to establish a Child Survival Fund within the U.S. foreign-aid program. We sought an initial $50 million for it. Congress responded to a flow of letters by approving the initiative and appropriating $25 million for it, plus another $65 million for related international health activities. Within a few years, funding for child survival had increased to $300 million.

The Rising of Bread for the World

Jim Grant was ecstatic. By this time Grant was director of UNICEF and had become the international champion of child survival. In this capacity he "probably saved more lives than were destroyed by Hitler, Mao and Stalin combined," wrote *New York Times* columnist Nicholas Kristof.* Grant would almost certainly have won the Nobel Peace Prize, had UNICEF not earlier received it. He called Bread for the World "the key citizen force in translating the idea of child survival into concrete action." He said that not only did Bread's work and Congress's action give child survival a boost, but this in turn triggered similar responses from other donor nations. By 2007 UNICEF reported that the number of young children dying each day of malnutrition and preventable diseases was down from 40,000 to 26,400—still deplorably high. But this remarkable change, which prevents 5 million deaths each year, occurred to a large extent because ordinary folks like you, who are reading this book, took a few minutes to write letters to their elected officials in Congress about child survival.

I asked Grant, "How much money does it take, on average, to save a child's life?" He said $500 saves a life, and that does not include other health benefits, such as preventing children from going blind or suffering other long-term disabilities. At $500 a life, $300 million would save the lives of 600,000 young children. This was happening year after year from U.S. funding alone, and by 2008 the U.S. foreign-aid account for child health and survival had grown to $1.7 billion. Aid of this kind has introduced changes that have become standard practice in many poor countries, and hundreds of millions of struggling parents are now familiar with simple things they can do to keep their children from dying. I think it is pretty clear that for each letter written to a member of Congress in support of child survival, dozens and more likely hundreds of lives have been saved. Yet we are prone to think, "What I do won't make any difference."

In July 1986, the *American Journal of Public Health* published an article entitled (I am not kidding) "Lobbying for International Health: The Link between Good Ideas and Funded Programs: Bread for the World and the Agency for International Development." The authors, two MDs from the Department of International Health at Johns Hopkins University, were prompted to investigate the reasons

* Nicholas D. Kristof, "Good News: Karlo Will Live," in the *New York Times*, March 6, 2008.

for an unprecedented increase of 60 percent in the U.S. Agency for International Development's international health account in 1985. They concluded that the main reason was the work of Bread for the World in generating tens of thousands of letters to Congress for the Child Survival Fund and related health-care activities. The article described in detail some of the twists and turns the legislation took at various stages in Congress, how the staff and members of Bread responded, and how the legislation passed despite opposition from the Reagan administration. The article also noted that previous efforts by the Carter administration, Senator Hubert Humphrey, and various organizations to increase funding for international health had failed to gain congressional support. The writers concluded: "Close examination of the legislative history demonstrates that direct, focused and organized constituent pressure was almost certainly what turned congressional indifference into broad-based support."

Bread for the World's success with child survival abroad brings to mind success in our own country with the nutrition program for Women, Infants, and Children (see chapter 12), a different form of child survival. These two programs rank among the major legislative achievements of Bread during the 1970s and 1980s.

Women in Development

In 1988 Bread policy analyst Lane Vanderslice proposed legislation to require better implementation and stronger support for "Women in Development." The U.S. Agency for International Development's evaluation of its own work revealed pathetic neglect of women. To cite an example, it said this about one of its projects in Thailand: "Project management assumed that men were the principal farmers and trained them to carry out crop trials. In reality, many men had outside income sources and were frequently away from the farm. Because wives of farmers received no training, crops were planted incorrectly and did not grow...and a nitrogen-fixing crop intended to fertilize rice did not get planted." Women were never consulted about their part in the project and as a result it failed.

Lane came up with the ingenious idea of putting into proposed legislation the agency's own recommendations, which advocated the

135

inclusion of women in every phase of its work. That idea found sponsors in Congress and it became the object of our Offering of Letters campaign in 1988. The agency promptly opposed the bill—it fought its own recommendations!

The staff had a harder time than usual getting members excited about this campaign because it seemed "off mission." Some asked, "Why are we working on the issue of women?" The question gave us an opportunity to explain how discrimination against women—far more extreme in most poor countries than in the United States—is a big cause of hunger. Even today—

- Women produce most of the food for family use and local consumption in Africa and Asia, but most of the planning and execution of agricultural aid projects (and other types of projects, for that matter) are handled by men.
- Nearly two-thirds of the world's 774 million adult illiterates are women.
- Most of the 72 million children of primary school age without access to basic education are girls.
- Impoverished women given opportunities to enhance their income almost always provide better nutrition, health care, and education for their families. That is much less true of men.
- The World Bank has said that of all the issues related to poverty in developing countries, the single most critical intervention is the education of girls.

Our campaign helped to get the *Women in Development* bill enacted. It required that all U.S. aid projects include women at every stage, from conception and planning, to execution and evaluation. The cost of doing this is small, but the aid benefits more people. The legislation has influenced other aid agencies, as well as recipient country governments, to do the same. Though not a headline grabber, it has pushed forward the frontier of opportunity for countless struggling girls and women, and in so doing quietly contributes to the reduction of hunger.

Trying to Harvest Peace

On March 27, 1989, a small article at the bottom of the front page of *The New York Times* caught my attention. Election returns in President Mikhail Gorbachev's own voting district in Moscow had produced a stunning surprise: Ilya Zaslavsky, a twenty-nine-year-old research scientist with artificial legs, had beaten the Communist Party candidate (a prominent television commentator) for a seat in the new Congress of People's Deputies. Gorbachev's policy of *glasnost* ("openness") did not allow for an opposition party, but for the first time it did permit independent candidates to run. Though most seats were not contested, a majority of those that were contested resulted in defeat for Communist candidates—an unthinkable development. The fig leaf of popular support for the Communist Party had fallen.

I was elated. It seemed to me that this signaled the beginning of the collapse of Soviet Communism. Subsequent events produced mounting evidence of a likely collapse and led eventually to the dismantling of the Berlin Wall. Meanwhile I began writing another book, *Harvesting Peace: The Arms Race and Human Need,*° as Bread for the World prepared to launch a major campaign in 1990 that we called *Sharing the Harvest of Peace*. Envisioning the demise of the Cold War, it called for an end to the arms race, along with a shift of resources and energy toward peaceful development.

We sensed a truly huge opportunity at a moment of historic change. Such moments rarely last long. People were beginning to talk about a peace dividend, though we preferred to depict a harvest. A dividend evokes the image of business profits for a few, while a harvest suggests benefits for everyone.

In collaboration with Senator Mark Hatfield (R-OR), and Representative Matt McHugh (D-NY) and others, Bread for the World helped draft the *Harvest of Peace Resolution*, which was introduced in the U.S. House and Senate in early 1990. The gist of it was that the world has "an unprecedented opportunity to reverse the $1 trillion arms race and promote peaceful development." It stated that it is the

---

° Arthur Simon, *Harvesting Peace: The Arms Race and Human Need* (Kansas City, MO: Sheed & Ward, 1990).

sense of Congress "that the United States should help achieve common security by reducing the world's reliance on the military and redirecting resources to peaceful efforts toward overcoming hunger and poverty and meeting basic human needs."

The resolution proposed seven specific actions and concluded by saying, "It is the further sense of the Congress that the United States should make fostering of common security [through implementation of these actions] a primary foreign and domestic policy objective."

Passage of that resolution became the objective of our campaign in 1990, and it generated an unusually large response. As messages to members of Congress mounted, so did sponsors of the resolution. Nationally prominent experts from both parties, including key figures from no less than six previous administrations, endorsed it.* Before long 25 senators and 173 representatives had cosponsored it, and prospects for eventual passage looked promising. A reduced threat, we argued, meant that money was already available for peaceful development. Old habits and entrenched interests resist change, however, and the administration's proposed budget for 1991 asked, in effect, that the peace dividend be spent on the Pentagon. But we seemed to be winning this argument in Congress.

Then in August of 1990 Iraq seized Kuwait. The Gulf crisis precipitated a war to free Kuwait and altered the mood in Congress, so the resolution never reached the floor of either house for a vote. History had opened a promising door for a brief moment, but events conspired to close it. I recalled a question that theologian John Howard Yoder had asked of us at several Bread for the World seminars: "Are you prepared for failure?" He meant that setbacks are inevitable, and what God requires of us is not success but faithfulness. Clearly this was a setback, though I do not believe for a moment that the campaign was a wasted effort, because we prodded national leaders and many others to think seriously about turning swords into plowshares, a hope that must be kept alive. More important, Christians place their ultimate hope not in anything so fleeting as shifting political winds, but in the resurrection of Jesus.

That keeps us going even when the tide turns momentarily against us.

---

* Harvest of Peace Resolution, p. 170.

15

Changing of the Guard

The Harvest of Peace Resolution was not without some immediate benefits. It made an impact on the thinking and voting of members of Congress, and served as a rallying point for our agenda. The Senate Appropriations Committee sent a strong message of support for some of the resolution's principles in its report to the full Senate regarding foreign-aid funding. However, our campaign alarmed military-industrial interests, which have political clout in every state and most congressional districts. Administration and congressional leaders agreed to make modest cuts in military spending, but to prevent future military cuts from being transferred to human-needs programs. This agreement, enacted by Congress, built a firewall of sorts against further defense reductions.

At the outset we announced that the Harvest of Peace Resolution would be the first part of a three-year Share the Harvest of Peace Campaign. Our second year focused on *The Horn of Africa Recovery and Food Security Act of 1991*, which became the target of our Offering of Letters that year and was enacted in April 1992. It helped stir the State Department to chair peace negotiations in Ethiopia, where an orderly transition to a new government spared many thousands from violence and hunger. The bill secured additional aid for famine recovery and peaceful development in a distressed region of Africa that includes Ethiopia, Somalia, and Sudan. It also discouraged further military aid to governments in that region, which had been armed by the United States and the Soviet Union during the Cold War.

A similar effort helped shift funds from military aid to demobilization and peacekeeping for impoverished El Salvador, where a decades-long civil war brought torture and often death to tens of thousands of Salvadorans, as well as displacement of more than a million people.

139

By the spring of 1992, Bread could report that, adjusted for inflation, U.S. defense spending since 1989 had dropped 14 percent.

My Decision to Retire

My sabbatical in 1985 had given me time to begin reflecting about my future and the future of Bread for the World. Upon my return, I told the board of directors that arguably the most important single thing I could do for Bread in the years ahead was to pave the way for my successor. In the spring of 1990, as our Harvest of Peace Campaign was beginning to take hold, I told the board that I planned to step aside the following year and asked that they begin planning for a new chief executive. Our board chair, Father Bill Byron, SJ, who in 1972 had served on Bread's organizing committee and was by this time president of the Catholic University of America, took the lead in establishing a committee and setting up a process for the search.

I based my decision to leave on several factors: Counting the start-up years, I had been at it for two decades. That's a long time, and I wanted to leave while I was still active and not when others decided I had stayed too long. I was beginning to feel that I had carried Bread about as far as I could, and that my creative juices were not flowing as freely as they used to. The qualities that founders usually bring to a movement or organization (and Bread is a combination of both) are seldom the same qualities that are needed for later stages of growth, and I did not consider myself an exception. Bread's paid membership had leveled off at about 42,000. It seemed to me that a more prominent role on the national scene would require fresh leadership with professional skills that exceeded my own. I also looked forward to spending more time with my family and having more time to write. Qualified leaders were evident in the antihunger movement, and I was confident that Bread could attract strong candidates.

I asked the board to do two things before the arrival of my successor. The first was to set up endowments for Bread for the World and for Bread for the World Institute, so we could build a stronger financial base for our mission in years to come. The second was to revisit our needs-based salary policy. It was important that our salary policy be revised while I was still serving as president, because we needed to raise professional- and management-level salaries. These would take effect after I left, so I could push for a new policy without any suspicion that I was trying to benefit myself. In addition, I thought a change in policy would enable us to attract a stronger set of candidates to replace me.

Setting up the mechanism for endowments was easy, but changing the salary policy was an emotionally charged issue for many staff members. We were blessed to have on our board Bishop Francis Murphy, who had experience doing this for the Catholic Archdiocese of Baltimore. He was a gentle, thorough man, who sensed the importance of making the change, as well as the need to build confidence among staff and board members for it.

As I indicated in chapter 9, our policy from the very beginning was to pay staff members on the basis of need, not position. That seemed consistent with our mission as a Christian movement working against hunger. It also served the practical purpose of enabling us to hire our initial staff without much money in the bank. The salary policy proved to be popular with our members, who saw it as evidence of integrity, a sign that we were truly committed to hungry people, and were captive to Jesus and not the culture. And it attracted staff members with a high level of commitment to Bread's mission.

For these reasons the policy served us well for a number of years. But difficulties began to emerge. When determining salaries, you have to trust others to be fair in presenting their need—though we did develop guidelines. As I look back, I am surprised that this freedom was seldom abused, or so it seems to me. Still, one person's need is another's luxury, so "need" can be quite subjective. As the staff grew larger, it became more difficult to administer this policy consistently and fairly, and disparities mounted. Rumbles of discontent began to surface as people noticed real or imagined inequities.

In addition, the policy sometimes prevented us from hiring highly qualified persons, because our salaries for positions that required advanced education and skilled leadership were far below standard. I am proud of our staff members and profoundly grateful for their dedication and professionalism. But there were occasions when we lost the opportunity to bring an exceptional talent to Bread, simply because that person's financial need (or expectation) was beyond our range and would have undermined our policy.

It was also the case that, because staff members with limited skills were usually getting higher wages than they could earn elsewhere, a few who were not all that happy or productive at Bread stayed longer than was good for them or for us. So with respect both to those with limited skills and those with more complex skills, our policy caused problems.

For these reasons the liabilities of the policy began to overshadow its advantages, and it became clear to me that the mission of Bread would be better served by shifting to a modified needs-based policy that came closer to market realities. So after a detailed study, including input from each staff member, the board approved a proposal along that line.

Some staff members who received raises under the new system objected vigorously. Imagine that! They didn't want higher salaries. They were committed to the needs-based policy and felt the change was abandoning part of the soul of Bread. But our salary policy had to be mission-driven, and that mission now required a new policy.

David Beckmann Elected

As it turned out, I knew the three finalists who were interviewed by the board to take my place, all three of them exceptional leaders with distinguished records. The board chose David Beckmann, an economist at the World Bank who also served on our board of directors. In September 1991, he became Bread for the World's second president.

The fact that David had spent fifteen years with the World Bank alarmed some staff and board members, and no doubt others, who feared that he would bring a top-down, bureaucratic mentality to the job. They were unaware of the track record he had at the bank as an innovator who was forever coming up with new ideas, constantly challenging the bank to engage grassroots organizations and pay more attention to reducing poverty at the local level.

I first got to know David when he started at the bank and became active in Bread for the World. He had accomplished a lot before joining the bank. Born and raised in Lincoln, Nebraska, he graduated with honors from Yale and got a Master of Divinity degree from Christ Seminary (Seminex), St. Louis, in 1974, the year Bread for the World was launched nationally. He had already worked in several inner-city neighborhoods and had spent a year in Ghana, West Africa, studying indigenous Pentecostal churches. In 1975 he received a graduate degree from the London School of Economics. He was ordained as a missionary-economist (perhaps the only one in captivity) and did rural development work in Bangladesh for the Lutheran World Federation until the World Bank discovered him.

At the bank David worked on slum improvement, low-cost housing, and microenterprise promotion in East Africa and Latin America, until he was promoted to write speeches for the president of the World Bank for several years. He badgered the bank to focus more sharply on poverty reduction by working with nongovernmental organizations, including religious, environmental, and community groups. So the bank put him in charge of a new unit to expand those ties in developing countries. Over the years he traveled and worked in seventy different countries. He had also written a few books and for ten years led a weekly seminar that he started at the bank for discussing spiritual values and development. Along the way he married Janet Williams, and by the time he arrived at Bread they had added two sons, Andrew and John.

When I announced my decision to retire, David was on track to become one of the bank's country representatives. At age forty-three he had become a rising star at the bank, with his career on an upward trajectory. But David was so convinced of the impact Bread for the World could make in reducing hunger that he put his hat in the ring as a candidate to become Bread's next president for a small fraction of the salary he was already earning.

David brought an extraordinary range of strengths to the position, including administrative skills and a deep faith. Christian faith informed his role as an economist devoted to poverty reduction. In his first message to Bread members, he wrote: "The Gospel of God's love for us in Jesus Christ can motivate political change against hunger on the necessary scale. No other social force is likely to do so."

The Rising of Bread for the World

David invited me to join him on trips to Chicago and New York to visit key people and hold a couple of press conferences. One pleasant surprise of those trips was meeting Christine Vladimiroff, a Benedictine sister who had just started her new job as chief executive of *Feeding America* (formerly America's Second Harvest), the umbrella agency for most of the nation's food banks. David thought *Feeding America* could play a much stronger role in addressing hunger if food banks and their local networks would advocate for more enlightened government policies. To our surprise, before we could even introduce the idea, Christine announced that she intended to move *Feeding America* in that direction. I subsequently served on its board for six years, and I know she excelled as its CEO. She got *Feeding America* to include advocacy within its orbit, and it has become more active in pressing the federal government to do its part in ending hunger here at home.

David's approach to *Feeding America* signaled an initiative that would become a mark of his leadership at Bread: an effort to persuade people and organizations engaged in direct assistance to help "transform the politics of hunger" by calling upon the U.S. government to secure justice for hungry people, and not to use private assistance as an excuse for ducking its responsibility. As for Christine, after ten years of leading *Feeding America*, she became prioress of her Benedictine community in Erie, Pennsylvania, joined Bread's board of directors, and chaired it with distinction for several years.

At David's request, the board of directors gave me permanent status as president emeritus. I'm grateful for the opportunity to continue serving, but I told David I would stay away from meetings for a year so he could make improvements in administration and discuss problems freely with the board without anyone having to worry about offending me.

I've heard frequent stories of tension between the founder of an organization and the CEO who replaced him or her, but I have to say that in this case the transition was entirely happy. That is true partly because David has been gracious and thoughtful in involving me in Bread's efforts, but mainly because his exceptional leadership has made Bread for the World a much stronger and more effective instrument against hunger. That has been a joy to behold.

Christian Children's Fund

With David Beckmann ready to take my place at Bread for the World, Paul McCleary, president of the Christian Children's Fund (CCF), asked if I would open and direct a Washington office for that Richmond-based organization. I knew Paul from his years as executive director of Church World Service, by far the largest entity of the National Council of Churches, and had high respect for him. I had served on the Church World Service oversight committee during that time and traveled to Vietnam and West Africa at Paul's request. His job offer attracted me, but I first investigated the work of CCF and the way in which it handled child sponsorships to make sure I could confidently give part of my life to it. I was impressed with what I learned, and in the fall of 1991, I joined the staff, while still remaining active with Bread.

The next six years gave me a chance to see from the inside the work of a large charitable antipoverty organization. This included visiting projects in East Africa and Ecuador, trips memorable because of the people who gave me a glimpse of their hope and determination in the face of adversity. Nothing makes CCF come so vividly to life as direct contact with its sponsored children and their families.

I had a close brush with death in Uganda, when the van in which I was riding suddenly skidded out of control at high speed in a heavy rain, flew into a ditch, and went tumbling. Miraculously, all seven of us climbed out with minor injuries, which is more than I can say for the van. I spent the most painful night of my life, and maybe the happiest one, indescribably grateful to be alive. As Winston Churchill once observed, "There is nothing so exhilarating as being shot at and missed." When I returned home and said bedtime prayers with my five-year-old daughter Leah, I told her I wanted to thank God for being so good to me in sparing my life. "Yes," she reminded me, "but God would have been good to you even if you had died." Although I still get occasional aches from that accident, I accept them as signals from God not to take life for granted.

Thanks to Christian Children's Fund staff member John Williamson, who did one of the earliest reports on AIDS orphans, I had become aware of the devastation that AIDS was beginning to cause in Africa, for which Uganda was then the epicenter, and the burgeoning number of children left behind. The purpose of the trip on the day of the accident was to visit the Rakai district, where AIDS was first discovered and where the HIV-AIDS virus may have originated. The district was rife with children orphaned by the disease, and I wanted to see the innovative work that World Vision was doing there in response to AIDS. Although that trip was aborted, I did visit many children in Kenya and Uganda orphaned by AIDS. In one case I had the privilege of conversing with a mother who lay near death on the floor of her hut and who was seeking the consolation of the Gospel. Her oldest son, age seventeen, had already assumed responsibility of caring for three younger children. Some of the saddest faces I have ever seen were those of grandmothers who in their old age were caring for their dead children's children, despite their own extreme poverty.

When I returned, John and I invited representatives of other private aid organizations to form an AIDS Orphans Task Force, which met periodically in Washington to share information on developments in the field. I think it served the useful purpose of keeping agencies better informed. A handful of us almost succeeded in launching an ambitious interagency project for the planning and coordination of work related to HIV-AIDS in Africa, but in the end the complications of getting various large and busy agencies to focus sufficiently on this proved beyond our reach.

Much of my work for the Christian Children's Fund involved reporting to its headquarters on a great variety of meetings or briefings with other agency representatives, some of them at the State Department or the World Bank, to keep us abreast of developments or to explore possible opportunities for new projects. Sometimes foreign visitors provided the occasion for these. One such visitor was the deputy foreign minister of North Korea, who appealed to our agencies for aid to his self-isolated, famine-stricken country, while simultaneously assuring us that the country would get along fine without us, if necessary. This happened during a period in which two-million North Koreans were dying of starvation. The country was desperate for help, but impeded it by resisting the monitoring of aid.

I came to admire my colleagues at CCF and other agencies, and I learned much from them. The thing that I hoped most to achieve, however, eluded me. I wanted to convince CCF to become more engaged in advocacy for children. I think McCleary had that in mind when he hired me, but he left the organization before we could bring it about. Ironically, as one of the agencies to receive child survival funds from the U.S. government, CCF reaps benefits from Bread for the World's work. But at the time, few agencies wanted to risk alienating their donors by asking them to contact members of Congress to expand the government's role in assisting people abroad. I think the fear was misplaced. More important, if an agency's mission is to give needy children basic care and opportunity, that mission should extend beyond its own institutional programs. An organization like CCF could use its experience and well-deserved credibility with 350,000 child sponsors and donors to inform them of proposals before Congress that would move the entire nation to do more to help the world's children. Even urging their donors to do this once a year on one key issue and receiving a 10 percent response would prompt our nation's leaders to take bolder action against global hunger and poverty. Many of the 26,400 young children who now die each day might live.

16

Transforming the Politics of Hunger

When David Beckmann began to lead us in 1991, Bread for the World faced a difficult political environment made possible by the widespread public tolerance of hunger. Not that few people cared about hunger—millions of Americans were involved with churches and agencies engaged in direct assistance—but few Americans saw the connection between hunger and national policies. The result was a passive, almost fatalistic acceptance of a certain level of hunger as inevitable. Because they sensed little pressure from their voters, presidents and members of Congress settled for half-way measures. David saw the need for Bread to ratchet up efforts to arouse the public and the nation's leaders in order to change the politics that tolerated hunger.

This political environment was greatly aggravated by tax cuts in the 1980s that benefited primarily the well-to-do. These cuts, along with surges in military spending, led to vast, unprecedented peace-time budget deficits that measured in the hundreds of billions of dollars each year. As a result, mounting deficits continued far into the 1990s and created pressure to cut costs elsewhere. The simplistic myths popularized by President Reagan that "government is the problem, not the solution," and that tax cuts would pay for themselves, had taken hold, despite evidence to the contrary. For many in the administration and in Congress, tax cuts were a way of creating a financial crisis that would force the reduction of government spending. Domestic antipoverty programs provided the easiest target. As government assistance shrank, more people began turning to food pantries and soup kitchens for emergency help, and the number of those agencies grew from a handful in 1980 to about 42,000 by 1990.

Because budget deficits had become an excuse for asking hungry Americans to tighten their belts, Bread for the World continued to campaign vigorously during the 1990s to defend nutrition programs against cuts and urged that they instead be improved and expanded. The portion of Americans below the poverty line had risen from 11.1 percent in 1973 to 15 percent in 1993. That year Bread's *Every Fifth Child* campaign (highlighting that 20 percent of the nation's children lived in poverty) helped win almost $2 billion in increases for the Women, Infants, and Children nutrition program, Head Start, and Job Corps. The following year our *A Child Is Waiting* resolution rallied support for another $260 million for the nutrition program, giving much needed assistance to an additional 350,000 young children and pregnant mothers. Bread worked for gains in the food stamp and other nutrition programs as well, helping to restore some of the cuts from the 1980s.

Polarized Politics

During this time the nation was becoming more polarized politically. Politics, the art of compromise, became uncompromising. Fewer members of Congress were willing to reach across party lines. Caustic remarks replaced civility. Campaign ads became increasingly negative and sometimes vicious. By its own quarreling Congress seemed determined to demonstrate that government *is* the problem. Not surprisingly, public confidence in both government and the Congress began to sink. None of this helped hungry people or made Bread for the World's work easy.

In 1994 the public voted its opinion of Congress by turning the Democrats out and giving Republicans a solid majority in both the House and the Senate. Republicans had proposed a new "Contract with America" that, among other things, promised sweeping changes in the welfare program. In his 1992 campaign for the presidency, Bill Clinton had promised "to end welfare as we know it," but postponed action on that in order to put his energy behind health-insurance coverage. That turned out to be a costly political mistake. While the health measure was faltering during the 1994 campaign, Republicans seized the initiative on welfare reform, which had strong public support. The 1996 bill that Congress subsequently passed and Clinton signed contained tough requirements to force many people off welfare, but gave them limited help (such as job training and child care) for making the transition. The legislation worked better than its critics feared, because it promoted personal responsibility, but worse than its backers promised, because it aimed more at cutting costs than moving people out of poverty.

The welfare law helped many people, but dealt a severe blow to others. It cut $54 billion from antipoverty programs, including food assistance, and barred almost a million legal immigrants from food stamps. But Bread played a key role in preventing the food stamp program from being turned over to the states, where it would have been subject to very divergent and lower levels of funding. Bread also responded with a *Hunger Has a Cure* campaign the following year that, in coalition with others, was able to win back funding increases of $1.7 billion for nutrition programs. And in 1998 the coalition succeeded in restoring the most vulnerable legal immigrants—children, elderly, and the disabled—to the food stamp program (renamed in 2008 as SNAP, or Supplemental Nutrition Assistance Program), along with an $818 million increase in funding. SNAP, the backbone of food security for most poor people, still felt the squeeze of earlier cuts. But we kept inching the WIC nutrition program closer toward the 2008 level of $6 billion in assistance for more than 8 million young Americans.

During the late 1990s, gains in nutrition modified, but did not erase, the cuts of 1996, and each gain required us to struggle against determined opposition. Without Bread's grassroots network and the efforts of others in the coalition, however, many more Americans would have been made hungry or hungrier.

Hunger Abroad

The nation was doing no better in responding to hunger and poverty abroad. The end of the Cold War gave many members of Congress an excuse, however foolish, for cutting foreign aid. Poverty-focused foreign aid also declined. Bread continued to fight for improvements and adequate funding for it. Despite the downward trend, sometimes we made gains and sometimes our efforts fended

off cuts. Either way we kept alive a special focus on Africa and awareness of its needs.

Occasionally a single action proved decisive. In March 1992 the
Horn of Africa Recovery and Food Security Act, which pushed famine
relief, development, and peace in that region (see chapter 15) and for
which we had garnered broad support in Congress, was languishing on
the desk of Rep. Dante Fascell (D-FL) of Miami, who chaired the
House Foreign Affairs Committee. It was mired in a foreign aid bill on
which Congress could not agree. Bread activist Peter England visited
the editor of *The Miami Herald*, which responded with an editorial,
"Pass Horn of Africa Bill," calling on Fascell to bypass the foreign aid
bill and move it forward as a free-standing bill. That got his attention,
and the committee soon sent the bill to the full House for approval. The
Senate also approved and the bill became law.

Bread worked hard those years to oppose cuts in poverty-focused
aid, as, for example, in our 1995 campaign, *Africa: Crisis to Opportunity*.
We also sought improvements and funding increases to help small-scale
farmers and rural communities, and were able to get passed the 1998
Africa: Seeds of Hope Act, which halted a decline in funding for agricultural assistance. And in 2000 we helped shape and get Congress to pass
the *African Growth and Opportunity Act*, which has increased trade
and investment opportunities for a number of African countries, while
promoting free market reforms. Whether defending against cuts or
pressing for more and better aid and trade, Bread's work kept body and
hope alive for many very poor people.

During these years, Bread for the World Institute played a leading role in a coalition that was able to persuade the World Bank to
focus more sharply on poverty reduction and make democratic consultation with community-based organizations standard procedure
for its projects. These reforms opened the way for Bread to help
obtain further U.S. funding for the bank's work in poor countries.

Until the 1998 *Africa: Seeds of Hope Act* passed, our best efforts
cushioned, but could not prevent, the long decline in U.S. assistance
to poor countries. And as aid declined, more of it went for emergency
relief and less for the kind of assistance that could bring lasting gains
against hunger and poverty, such as helping struggling farmers produce more food. During the peak of U.S. aid to Europe under the
Marshall Plan after World War II, when the United States was far less

prosperous than it is today, our country contributed almost 3 percent of its total annual income, and 10 percent of its federal budget, to help desperate Europeans. But by the 1990s, our share of humanitarian and development assistance to poor countries had dropped to one-tenth of one percent of the nation's income—proportionately thirty times less—and to less than one half of one percent of the federal budget. Yet polls showed that Americans thought it to be about 15 to 20 percent of the budget. Measured as a percentage of national income, U.S. aid ranked at the very bottom of aid-giving nations; too few people knew this or understood its impact on poverty-stricken people.

The political will to end hunger was still in short supply. And David was determined to do something about it.

Building a Larger Movement

During my years as its president, Bread for the World worked with other groups, often joining and frequently leading coalitions for legislative campaigns. That took a modest amount of my time. But David saw more clearly than I did the opportunity to build a much larger, stronger movement against hunger, so he put substantially more time and energy into making it happen. As a result, Bread expanded and strengthened its ties with churches and religious groups, as well as a wide range of other organizations.

David's first message to Bread for the World's members laid the foundation for this. He noted that presidential debates and State of the Union speeches seldom if ever mentioned hunger, because politicians had the impression that government action to help hungry people is not popular among U.S. voters. "Despite our nation's lavish wealth," he wrote, "we have convinced ourselves that we cannot afford supplemental food for hungry children. What does this say about U.S. Christianity?" He added that Bread for the World and the entire hunger movement needed to become much stronger in order to achieve reforms that could bring an end to widespread hunger in this country and abroad.

"One of my ideas," he wrote, "is that Bread for the World reach out to private agencies that directly serve poor people." He noted that thousands of soup kitchens, food pantries, and other agencies—most of them church-related—were giving food to hungry people in U.S. communities. Another set of agencies assist poor people in developing countries. "I hope to augment Bread for the World's resources by urging and helping hunger service agencies to join us in lobbying the U.S. Congress." Bread for the World could not by itself summon the nation's will to end hunger, he said. We could play a key role, perhaps even a catalytic role, in bringing this about, but the public outcry that is needed almost certainly requires that many of the several million volunteers who contribute time or money to help hungry people also begin appealing to the nation's decision makers for the government to do its part.

After a series of consultations on this and many personal contacts by David, a number of private organizations doing relief and development overseas either began or expanded efforts to influence national policies. Others started to think about it. Interaction, an association to which most of them belong, gave strong encouragement through its own advocacy. But the real power lies in each organization arousing its own constituents to take action. More of this is beginning to happen, though much remains to be done.

Regarding hunger in our own country, nearly all of the major charitable networks that assist poor people, such as Catholic Charities and the Salvation Army, are advocating better policies. Food banks and pantries are especially important partners in speaking out for government nutrition programs. And the churches increasingly encourage members to show compassion for those who hunger by expressing their views to those who govern the nation.

If reading about this makes you yawn, I beg you to realize that ending hunger depends in no small part upon these groups and their people crying out to the nation's decision makers. It helps a lot when an organization speaks out. But it is a thousand times more powerful when their constituents do so as citizens and as voters.

If enough of us begin to insist, the United States could end most hunger within its borders within a year or two, and at relatively modest cost, simply by improving existing food-assistance programs and fully covering all citizens and legal immigrants who qualify for them. And over the long haul—through such things as education, job training, job creation incentives, and expansion of tax credits for the working poor—the nation could bring many more unemployed adults into the work force at wages that would lift them above the need for further assistance.

Globally as well, David said, citizens must sound the alert for the United States to provide much stronger leadership for making headway against hunger, poverty, and disease. The nation promised to help make this happen when it pledged to do its part in reaching the UN Millennium Development Goals, the first of which is to cut extreme hunger and poverty in half by 2015. An average of a penny a day per American would release a billion dollars a year for this purpose. The cost of a $2 ice-cream cone a week would add $30 billion. So the problem is not that cutting hunger and poverty costs too much. Generous and carefully targeted efforts are well within the capacity of the richest nation in history. These efforts would return both social and economic benefits to us far exceeding the additional cost, an amount equal to about 5 percent of our annual military spending.

If people already helping to relieve hunger and poverty through their own charitable aid realized these things and were moved to demand action from our president and the Congress, we could give hope to a host of hungry people.

The ONE Campaign and the Alliance to End Hunger

Acting on these ideas during the 1990s, Bread for the World built on them in the subsequent decade by helping to establish and participate in several new advocacy organizations. The most prominent of these is the ONE Campaign, an international antihunger movement proposed by Irish rock star Bono a few years after the Jubilee Debt Campaign, which I will soon describe. The ONE Campaign offers an easy way for people to register support for increasing, by one percent of the federal budget, what the nation contributes toward relieving poverty, hunger, and disease in poor countries. It has prompted tens of thousands of mainly young people to send an occasional e-mail to a member of Congress, boosting public support for increasing poverty-focused foreign aid. The ONE Campaign has also led a growing number of promising young leaders to more intensive involvement in Bread for the World, which will strengthen our efforts and the larger hunger movement for years to come.

Not as publicly prominent, but no less important, is the Alliance to End Hunger. One of Bread for the World's enduring strengths, the motivation of faith in Christ, brings with it also a limitation, because interest in and responsibility for ending hunger is not limited to Christians or even people of faith. Although Bread's Christian identity is clear, we have always welcomed people of any faith or no faith into our membership and have always worked in partnership with other groups, religious or secular, in order to get action from Congress or the White House. It is difficult, however, for most non-Christians to join a Christian organization, and off-limits for many secular entities to affiliate with one. So in 2001 David recommended to our board of directors that Bread take the lead in establishing a religiously neutral group made up of organizations from key sectors of society to join in fostering the political will to end hunger. For years he had argued that hunger is one problem we can solve, if we have the will to do it. Now he proposed bringing together companies, unions, universities, foundations, religious groups, private voluntary organizations, government agencies, and key individuals into the Alliance to End Hunger.

The alliance is now separately incorporated with its own board of directors. David serves as its president, and it is housed in Bread's headquarters on Capitol Hill. The alliance has built an impressive array of sixty members that include Feeding America, Auburn University, Cargill Foods, Mazon: A Jewish Response to Hunger, the Muslim Public Affairs Council, the National Farmers Union, Sodexho USA, the U.S. Conference of Catholic Bishops, and World Vision, as well as U.S. government and UN agencies with observer status. It has sponsored a series of polls that have been used to inform the media and elected officials that a large majority of the public favors effective government programs to help hungry people, and has worked with members of Congress and presidential candidates to encourage their leadership in this regard.

Alliance members share ideas and have found ways in which their own institutions can respond more adequately to hunger, with an emphasis on advocating better national policies. The alliance in this country encouraged the launch of the UN International Alliance against Hunger, and has served as one of the models for national alliances in twenty-five other countries. It also helped to launch Universities Fighting World Hunger, based at Auburn University in Alabama, which at this writing includes sixty colleges and universities. In these and other

155

ways the alliance is becoming an increasingly important partner with Bread for the World in transforming the politics of hunger.

In addition to strengthening the entire hunger movement in these ways, Bread for the World has also accelerated its own growth in membership, finances, and professional staff capability. These internal developments, in combination with a wide and growing spectrum of other voices that are being lifted on behalf of hungry people, raise the prospects for reaching that critical mass of public support that would enable both the nation and the world to overcome widespread hunger.

The Jubilee Debt Campaign

Near the turn of the millennium, a global campaign to cancel the indebtedness of some of the poorest countries of the world provided a dramatic example of what it would take to make the goal of ending hunger a compelling political force. It started with the concern of a few Christians in England about impoverished countries saddled with debts so staggering that many of their children could not afford to attend school. Health clinics were closing, and people were struggling desperately for food, clothing, and shelter. The Old Testament law concerning the year of Jubilee, when every fiftieth year, debts were forgiven, sparked an idea: Why not a *Jubilee Debt Campaign* to release the poorest countries from the burden of crushing debts to donor governments and international agencies—debts from loans often taken at the misguided urging of those donor nations and agencies. These countries would be forgiven their debts only under strict conditions to assure that the benefits would give opportunity to poor people. The idea caught on, and soon *Jubilee Debt Campaigns* were beginning to take hold in many countries.

In 1999 Bread for the World decided to make its Offering of Letters a campaign to get Congress to approve U.S. participation in Jubilee debt reduction. Bread for the World had helped get more than $2 billion in debt reduction for poor countries a decade earlier, but with a less-polarized, less cost-cutting Congress, and not as part of an international campaign. This time the stakes—and the obstacles— were far greater. When our board of directors voted for this campaign,

I remember thinking, "We've got to try, but it has little chance of succeeding with a Congress determined to slash programs." We had never tackled anything so big or more unlikely.

Bread was only one of many organizations supporting the campaign, which received its main impetus from churches and church leaders, including Pope John Paul II. Irish rock star Bono was so surprised to see nuns trumpeting the cause of debt reduction to help poor people that he had a faith-related conversion and put his mind as well as his popularity behind the campaign. Bread's role was crucial because we led the coalition that was responsible for developing legislation and getting Congress to approve it. We knew that without full U.S. participation, other donor nations would almost certainly lag in their support. And U.S. participation depended on persuading a resistant Congress.

Letters and e-mails began to flow. Jim Leach (R-IA), who chaired the House Banking Committee, surprised a group of Bread members who visited him by offering to become one of the chief sponsors—an unusual move for a committee chair. But Leach was known to be a moderate Republican, and we needed to make inroads among conservatives of both parties. One of the most conservative was Spencer Bachus (R-AL), new chair of the House subcommittee that had initial jurisdiction over the proposal. We feared that he might try to block its consideration, so we set out to persuade him. Bread members from his district mounted a campaign of letters and e-mails. A group of them visited him in Birmingham. Bachus admitted quite candidly that he knew little about the issue or the plight of people in poor countries, so he invited his Bread visitors to explain at length why debt reduction made good economic as well as moral sense. They left materials, including a copy of *Grace at the Table: Ending Hunger in God's World*, a book that David and I had recently written. The more he read about hunger and the suffering of poor people, the more he felt a sense of mission. Four of our members—Pat Pelham, Elaine van Cleave, Bobby Cardwell, and Roger McCullough—flew to Washington for a follow-up visit, carrying a petition signed by four hundred parishioners in Father Martin Muller's Our Lady of Sorrows Catholic Church.

On October 9, 1999, *The Washington Post* had a full-page feature entitled "GOP's Bachus Makes Debt Relief His Mission," reporting that he had astonished his colleagues in the House by championing a supposedly liberal cause. Spencer Bachus, a devout Southern Baptist, had become convinced that debt reduction was not only economically sound, but morally right, the kind of thing his Christian faith compelled him to espouse. He sent a letter to each of the other 434 members of the House, urging them to "please help 700 million of your brothers and sisters in the poorest countries." With each letter he enclosed $1.20 of his own money, the average cost per American for the first annual U.S. installment of the proposed debt relief. His support cleared the way for other conservatives to join him.

The Clinton administration, while favorably disposed, was holding back, not wanting to waste political capital on a losing issue. David visited Lawrence Summers, U.S. Secretary of the Treasury, who told him, "If Spencer Bachus is behind this, we better get going," and they did. In the end, even archconservative Senator Jesse Helms (R-NC) and evangelist Pat Robertson announced their support.

The bill eventually passed with a large bipartisan majority in both houses of Congress. After funding for it was also approved, David was asked to introduce President Clinton at the signing ceremony. Clinton gave Spencer Bachus credit for playing a crucial role, and David gave credit to our Birmingham members.

Bread's role is only one piece of a much larger story, of course. It took a combination of religious and secular leaders, a rock star, and a global grassroots movement. Many individuals and groups played key roles. Most of all, it depended upon the willingness of thousands upon thousands of ordinary folks to contact their own U.S. senators and representatives, without which all of the other efforts would have accomplished little. *The Jubilee Debt Campaign* demonstrated the kind of outcry from various quarters that is needed on an even-broader and more-sustained basis for mustering the political will to end hunger. But clearly that could be done.

The benefits of the debt campaign continue to grow. Putting in place the necessary conditions to qualify for debt reduction has strengthened democracy in poor countries, as nongovernmental organizations are consulted and given voice. As I write, twenty donor nations, along with the World Bank and the International Monetary Fund, have so far forgiven a total of $69 billion of virtually unrepayable debts, which gives poor countries almost $4 billion more each year for antipoverty initiatives. Largely as a result, 20 million more children in Africa are going to school, and families in thirty-three different countries have more food, better housing, and better health care; also, new small-scale enterprises are flourishing. In addition, the conditions required for debt forgiveness have brought about reforms that strengthen community organizations and local economies. Few of the millions who benefit will ever imagine that their newfound opportunity was made possible because a lot of ordinary Americans sent messages to members of Congress, urging a helping hand.

Besides directly benefiting millions of poor people, the *Jubilee Debt Campaign* shifted the political wind in the United States. By creating a more receptive mood for carefully targeted, poverty-focused aid to poor countries, it is helping to transform the politics of hunger.

9/11

The September 11, 2001, terrorist attack on the World Trade Towers and the Pentagon also had an impact on the politics of hunger. It led to the invasion of Afghanistan and was invoked, erroneously, as a reason for invading Iraq. President George W. Bush secured huge tax cuts (again benefiting mainly the well-to-do) that, in combination with the wars, caused our nation's annual deficit to soar—by $400 billion in 2008, and this was even before the economic meltdown and bailout. This left scant room to improve prospects for the nation's poor.

However, funding for nutrition programs jumped from $33 billion to $54 billion between 2000 and 2007—a remarkable 36-percent inflation-adjusted increase during the Bush administration. This happened in large part because growth in poverty drew more people into the food stamp program. But it also happened because the work of Bread and others was bearing fruit, and attitudes were beginning to change.

By 2008 the food stamp program no longer used stamps, but fraud-secure plastic cards, and was renamed SNAP (Supplemental Nutrition Assistance Program). Columnist Michael Gerson, former speech writer for Bush and a truly compassionate conservative, pointed to the cost of *not* preventing hunger, argued for reaching the qualified millions left out of SNAP, and wondered how the nation could justify funding only three weeks of food each month for hungry people.

The Rising of Bread for the World

The attack of 9/11 also had an effect on U.S. politics regarding hunger abroad. Because the subsequent decision to invade Iraq struck much of the world as arrogant, and because its execution was handled so poorly, world opinion of the United States plummeted. Out of this came a growing recognition that our country needed to do a much better job of winning the hearts and minds of people, and that it be seen not as a bully but as a friend of struggling people everywhere. At an international summit in March 2002, President Bush pledged that the United States would increase its assistance to some of the poorest nations by $5 billion a year and would reach that goal in three years. A special Millennium Challenge Account was set up with strict standards for the disbursement of that aid. The biggest piece of this commitment, however, was a $3 billion a year initiative (expanded to $4 billion a year in 2009) to combat HIV-AIDS in 15 targeted countries.

Bread for the World campaigned hard during the decade to increase poverty-focused development assistance, and partly as a result, U.S. funding for these programs more than doubled, from $6.8 billion in 2000 to $15.5 billion in 2008—the first large and sustained increase in decades. The Millennium Challenge Account, which Bread helped to shape and support, is part of that increase. As a result of these gains, U.S. aid to reduce poverty in Africa—though it started from a pathetically low base—has increased sixfold and includes substantial increases for agriculture and rural development. The combination of increased aid and trade, together with the reduced debt of poor countries, had much to do with the fact that, with notable exceptions, by 2007 the economies of most sub-Saharan African nations were growing, and hunger was receding. Unfortunately in 2008, the soaring cost of food and energy, and a mounting global recession, threatened those gains.

But here I am, throwing statistics and abstractions at you, when we should be thinking about people. Picture yourself—or your children—in the place of an impoverished child who finally has a chance to go to school, or a mother at last able to feed her family, or a father finally able to buy medicine. Think how life without such basic necessities would tear you apart, and how your spirits would rise if obtaining them suddenly became possible. Over the years I've seen many people in each situation, and the difference can either break your heart or make it soar.

That difference is why each of us needs to step up and do our part to change the politics of hunger.

17

Retrospect and Prospect

I retired from Christian Children's Fund in October 1997, still in good health and looking forward to additional time with my family and the chance to do more with Bread for the World. My idea of retirement was expressed perfectly by two Catholic nuns in their eighties, who were actively engaged with Bread in Fort Collins, Colorado. They were new to the city, and Sharon Johnson, a local Bread leader, asked one of them why they decided to retire in Fort Collins. She replied, "Oh, we didn't come here to retire. We came to celebrate!"

One way I celebrate my retirement is by encouraging people to include Bread for the World in their estate, because a stronger financial base greatly enhances our mission. We currently have several hundred members who have reported putting Bread in a trust, a will, an insurance policy, or an annuity. Legacies already give a modest but growing boost to our work each year, and some go into our growing endowments to strengthen us for years to come. Most of these legacies are small, others quite large; I value each of them. If each of our current 61,000 members bequeathed just $1,000 to Bread, it would eventually generate an additional $61 million toward ending hunger. I spend two months on the phone each year calling these legacy folks and thanking them for their very special part in Bread's mission. They are salt-of-the-earth people, many with life stories that have touched me deeply, often rising above their own personal adversity to care about those who go hungry.

Our donors also have a sense of humor. One worked for a prominent think tank, and I kept getting this voice message: "Hi, there! This is _____, the world's leading authority. I am too busy thinking great

161

thoughts to come to the phone right now." I tried many times to reach him, but he was always too busy thinking great thoughts.

I spend much of my time writing books, and I find that it's a good way to learn. I wrote my previous one, *Rediscovering the Lord's Prayer*,* because in midlife I woke up to the prayer's importance as a way of listening to God and putting my life more fully in God's presence. Retirement has allowed me more time for prayer and reflection. I regret that I was not wise enough to do much of this earlier in life, imagining myself to be too busy, when in reality I needed to approach my busy-ness with more insight and strength from God.

As I reflect on almost eight decades of life, I am profoundly grateful for the way in which God has given me opportunities beyond anything I ever imagined, and has surrounded me with people who made up for countless limitations. I have also been saddened by failure in marriage and regret not having done better as a father, because of the pain these have caused my children, who have brought me joy. All of this I lift up to a merciful God, trusting that because of Jesus, we live in forgiveness and hope. God's grace sets me free to press on with a thankful heart.

Along with a fascinating inner-city ministry and my work with Bread for the World, I enjoyed following my brother Paul's career, and occasionally helping it. In 1988 that included a brief run in the presidential primaries, where his chances depended on winning the Iowa caucuses. He came short of doing so by only 3 percent. At the time the polls showed him running second to Michael Dukakis in New Hampshire. An Iowa victory would have given him a surge and made the New Hampshire primary a two-way race, which Paul thought he could win. Paul completed two terms in the Senate, then started a still-flourishing public policy institute ("a *do* tank, not a think tank," he said) at Southern Illinois University. He died in December of 2003 and was buried on the 75th anniversary of his baptism. The apostle for whom he was named wrote that "we have been buried with him by baptism into death, so that, just as Christ was raised from the dead…, so we too might walk in newness of life" (Rom 6:4). My brother walked that life with a dogged determination

---

* Arthur Simon, *Rediscovering the Lord's Prayer* (Minneapolis, MN: Augsburg Books, 2005).

to help those who struggle because they have few of the opportunities most of us take for granted. His example remains a source of strength for me. Behind the scenes Paul also gave me and Bread for the World's agenda many a boost.

Along with my parents and my children, Paul and his family are among the exceptional blessings of my life. I am grateful for the opportunity to have traveled throughout the United States and in countries on every continent. I've gotten to know many people who were truly great in spirit, among them members of my New York parish whose struggles planted the seed that grew into Bread for the World, those who served with me on Bread's staff and board, and Bread members across the land whose faith still inspires them to seek justice for hungry people.

Looking Back

Looking back over Bread for the World's first thirty-five years, I am pleased to say that we remain clearly focused on our mission. The vision that I and our organizing committee had of attracting Christians across denominational and political lines to press the nation's leaders for policies to reduce hunger—that vision remains solidly intact. We have learned much along the way about how to do it. We have grown from a handful of people operating on a prayer and a shoestring to a nationally respected citizens' voice that generates several hundred-thousand personal messages to members of Congress each year and that does more lobbying on world hunger and poverty than any other organization in the country. Bread has a staff of one hundred, and an annual combined budget for Bread, the Bread for the World Institute, and the Alliance to End Hunger of $12 million in 2009. More important, our efforts have a leveraging effect, a multiplication of loaves, with one dollar of advocacy typically bringing more than $100 in benefits to hungry people. In addition to each year's achievement, gains carry over from year to year from Bread's previous work on child survival, the emergency grain reserve, humanitarian aid, and other anti-poverty initiatives. As a result, millions of lives have been saved and millions more lifted above poverty or at least to higher levels of decency within poverty. Along with this, I believe that many have seen the hand of God at work.

Bread for the World still faces the ongoing challenge of persuading people that it is not only permissible to convey our opinions to elected officials, but a privilege and responsibility to do so, and that with respect to hunger, doing so is a huge opportunity to express the love in action that is urged upon us throughout the Bible.

People are wary of becoming citizen advocates for many reasons. Some Christians feel it violates the separation of church and state, when in reality they are separating faith from life. Some find policy issues too complicated, others too controversial. Issues often seem abstract to people, and the work required may fail to give them the same immediate satisfaction as helping in a soup kitchen or contributing food and money for relief. Millard Fuller, founder of Habitat for Humanity, says people support anything you can take a picture of, like someone swinging a hammer. But it is hard to take a picture of public policy.

In all candor, perhaps our main reason for neglecting advocacy is that most of us are so caught up in pursuing our own comfort that we don't care that much whether or not others go hungry. Yet we may call ourselves followers of Jesus, who urged radical compassion and generosity toward them. Could reluctance reflect that we are observers rather than followers, that our hearts have not been deeply touched by the love of Christ and neighbor? If so, then Jesus' words in Matthew 25, that the way we respond to hungry people is our response to *him*, suggests that not only is their well-being at stake, but also our own.

I have long contended that Christians will become voices for the hungry if two conditions are met: first, they must be convinced that doing so is an important, God-pleasing way of loving others; second, they must see what a difference it makes for them. On both counts the case is becoming increasingly clear and is persuading a growing number of people.

The current politics of hunger reflects an abundance of greed and complacency, just as slavery and racial segregation did in previous centuries until a determined core of committed Christians and other compassionate patriots fought an uphill battle to awaken the conscience of a nation. We see it again today, as the rich and powerful cling to privileges at the expense of the poor and powerless. We have just had an example of it, as I write, in the farm bill enacted by the Congress in 2008, which allots billions of dollars in subsidies primarily to owners of large and prosperous farms, but does little to help struggling farmers or poor rural communities. Worse yet, these subsidies distort the market and force small-scale farmers in poor countries to compete with us at a disadvantage, which imposes hardships and often hunger on their families.

A coalition of Bread for the World and others launched a nearly successful effort to reform this system but were beaten largely because leaders of both parties in the House and Senate caved in to big-farm interests. However, we helped win substantial increases in funding for food stamps, food banks, rural development, conservation programs, and assistance to disadvantaged farmers. We also greatly increased public awareness of the abuses in U.S. farm policies, so we are much better positioned to reform those policies when they are next considered. But the subsidies enacted provide a snapshot of the grip that moneyed interests often have on the nation's decision makers, and illustrate the challenge that you and I face in order to change the politics of hunger. It can be changed, but only if enough of us feel some moral responsibility for injustices and have enough compassion to express our concerns to our elected officials. To remain silent is to support the continuation of hunger.

Looking Ahead

As Bread for the World celebrates its 35th year, I see signs of danger and signs of promise. The world as a whole has made dramatic strides against hunger in my own lifetime. When I was a boy, President Roosevelt used to talk about two-thirds of the world being hungry, a reasonable guess. By the time Bread for the World began in 1974 about 35 percent was chronically undernourished. That narrowed to about 15 percent, at least until very recently. My lifetime has been a period of release from a terrible oppression for most of the world's people.

There are clouds on the horizon, however. Among them is global warming, the impact of which seems certain to fall disproportionately on poor people. More immediately, another crisis emerged during

2008, as the growing prosperity of formerly poor people placed new demands on the world's energy and food supply, causing prices to rise and driving many other people into hunger. Then financial markets began to collapse and, as I write, a global recession seems almost certain to further erode gains against hunger and poverty.

How will we respond to all of this?

I am reminded that the Chinese word for *crisis* combines the characters for *danger* and *opportunity*. The present crisis poses great danger to many, but also gives us an opportunity as a nation, in concert with other nations, to seek the common good, which by definition includes poor people. Nothing is certain, of course. The direction our country takes depends in large part on individuals, like you the reader, to cry out to our leaders and urge them to do what is right in the sight of God for hungry people.

The political climate gives conflicting signals. The nation seems to be tilting more toward the nation's founding ideals of liberty and justice for all, in part as a reaction to widening income disparities in our country, and in part because terrorism has alerted us to the importance of responding to the suffering of people abroad. The election of President Barack Obama and a new Congress—who are both called upon to "fix" our broken economy and address other great needs—makes the years in front of us an opportune time for bold initiatives against hunger and poverty, both globally and in our own country. But if support for doing so cuts across party lines, so will resistance to it. We have to assume that elected officials will muster the wisdom and courage to act only if we make known to them in great numbers our conviction that hunger must end.

As political shifts occur, Bread for the World is poised to take advantage. Our reputation, along with our numbers, has steadily grown, and we are preparing to become a stronger, more visible influence. Bread's president, David Beckmann, is now a recognized figure in hunger and development circles internationally, with access to many key leaders. Our ties with church bodies have never been stronger, and through the Alliance to End Hunger, we are forging durable partnerships with secular institutions as well as other faith groups. Bono's ONE Campaign, of which Bread is a founding member, has drawn thousands of young people into a first-step commitment against world poverty and disease. Private assistance agencies are doing more advocacy and in some cases beginning to urge their donors to do so as well. The *Jubilee Debt Campaign* stands as a demonstration of what can be done when many players stir the public and move decision makers. These are encouraging developments.

The next few years may be a God-given moment for dramatic gains against hunger. We do not know. We can only seize the opportunities that God gives and pray fervently, as we are urged by Jesus, for an end to hunger: "Thy will be done on earth as it is in heaven.... Give us this day our daily bread." God has already brought most of the world's growing population out of hunger and is clearly inviting us to be part of furthering this exodus. Perhaps we will be called to struggle against new odds for decades, just as those who fought slavery and racial segregation struggled seemingly in vain for generations, keeping hope alive, until finally the barriers began to yield and justice emerged. We do not know the time for justice to emerge regarding hunger, but we do know that we are called in Christ to seek on this earth the love and justice of God for those who hunger.

Do not think for a moment that in saying this I have mistaken the Christian hope in the resurrection for earthly bread, spiritual rebirth for a bowl of stew. My faith, like that of Christians throughout the ages, is anchored in the saving, forgiving, atoning work of Jesus, whose resurrection gives promise of life with God that begins now and endures forever. But precisely because it is based on an eternal hope, that faith sets us free from a fearful attachment to things that are certain to pass away, and gives us courage to practice, however imperfectly, God's love for others. Eugene Carson Blake, who chaired Bread's board our first four years, put it well in a sermon based on John 6 and Jesus' feeding of the multitude. Blake entitled his sermon "Bread from Heaven and Bread for the World." It is not either/or, but both/and. The one who gives us life-giving bread from heaven also provides bread for the physical hunger of others and calls us to do the same. And one may hope that the work of Bread for the World will draw people to the source of love, so that people are filled not only with bread for the body, but with the Bread of Life as well.

In Reflection

What strikes me about Bread for the World is how ordinary people, working together, can make such a difference. That was certainly the case with me, pastor of a small inner-city church. My experience is one that I have heard Bread members from all over the country express again and again: "God laid the suffering of hungry people on my heart and called me to do something about it." First, one small step, then another, and then another. Each time doors opened, inviting further steps.

Those of us who started Bread had slender portfolios for doing so. Had we waited for people better equipped to step forward and take the lead, we would still be waiting. Our understanding and resources were limited, but hunger disturbed us, and we accepted that as a call to action. We began with a tiny seed of an idea, but the seed had life and, when planted, God gave it growth. The handful that grew in each congressional district has become, like Gideon's army, a powerful instrument of change out of proportion to its numbers.

My role as a founder of Bread for the World was that of a midwife. I was there to help assist in its birth. But never having assisted in such a birth, I relied on others who willingly took part with me in delivering and caring for that newborn. At every stage along the way the talents, commitment, and generosity of those who caught the vision have helped to nurture Bread for the World. The writing of this book has almost overwhelmed me with a realization of the gratitude, too-seldom expressed, that I owe them. On top of that, Bread has flourished under the leadership of my successor, David Beckmann. Bread is larger, more professionally equipped, and more influential than it was when I turned the reins over to him. As a result, the reasons for giving thanks and the numbers of those who deserve it continue to grow.

In short, I look back with a grateful heart for being an unlikely instrument in the creation of a new thing that I believe is a work of God. And I look forward to the further unfolding of that work.